a Wolters Kluwer business

MW00748916

ss to Business

Succession
Planning

3rd Edition 2006

Malcolm T. Scarratt,
MA, CFP, CLU, CHFC, TEP

CCH Canadian Limited
300-90 Sheppard Avenue East
Toronto Ontario
M2N 6X1
1 800 268 4522
www.cch.ca

Published by CCH Canadian Limited

Important Disclaimer: This publication is sold with the understanding that (1) the authors and editors are not responsible for the results of any actions taken on the basis of information in this work, nor for any errors or omissions; and (2) the publisher is not engaged in rendering legal, accounting or other professional services. The publisher, and the authors and editors, expressly disclaim all and any liability to any person, whether a purchaser of this publication or not, in respect of anything and of the consequences of anything done or omitted to be done by any such person in reliance, whether whole or partial, upon the whole or any part of the contents of this publication. If legal advice or other expert assistance is required, the services of a competent professional person should be sought.

Edited by:
Shlomo Kapustin

Library and Archives Canada Cataloguing in Publication

Scarratt, Malcolm, 1947–
    The advisor's guide to business succession planning / Malcolm T.
Scarratt. — 3rd ed.

ISBN 1-55367-560-6

Second ed. published under title: Business succession planning for financial
    advisors.

1. Business enterprises — Registration and transfers — Canada. 2. Family-owned
business enterprises — Canada — Succession. 3. Estate planning — Canada.
I. Scarratt, Malcolm, 1947– . Business succession planning for financial advisors.
II. Title.

KE1450.S32 2006   346.7105'2   C2006-904188-1
KF1382.S32 2006

© 2006, CCH Canadian Limited

Typeset by CCH Canadian Limited.
Printed in the United States of America.

P R E F A C E

A s the leading edge of the "baby boomers" moves closer to the age of retirement, or at least to the age of working less or working differently, the topic of business succession is becoming more and more important, as well as more and more urgent. Suddenly, the rebels who grew up in the 60's are in their 60's. The unprecedented growth in business values in recent years has accompanied the wave of the "boomers", so that the process of deciding how to handle succession and how to handle wealth is of greater interest and greater magnitude than at any previous time. In addition, tragic world events of the past few years have prompted many business owners to question their priorities. Focusing on personal and family issues will of necessity involve a closer analysis of choices and will provide added impetus to the business succession process.

The way in which our clients approach this transition will have a significant impact on the businesses they have built and on the next generation of owners, whether in a family business environment or otherwise, and the role of advisors to these businesses must encompass more than technical and tax expertise. The "people" issues will mean the difference between success and failure.

This book aims for a balance between the technical and the "people" issues, emphasizing neither at the expense of the other.

For simplicity, all tax calculations are based on a 40% personal marginal rate, a 20% small business rate, a 25% rate on dividends and an effective 20% tax rate on capital gains.

PREFACE TO THE THIRD EDITION

This edition of *The Advisor's Guide to Business Succession Planning* has two significant additions:

1) A chapter devoted to the succession planning process for financial advisors. We work with our clients to ensure their success in this area, but we all too often neglect our own plans. The objective of this chapter is to encourage financial advisors to begin the succession planning process by thinking about some of the key issues involved and considering how those issues might affect the organization, structure and conduct of a practice. Succession planning is rarely effective or efficient when done at the last minute — the earlier the process is considered, the more likely it is that the desired end result will come to pass.

2) A chapter devoted to looking at the succession planning process through the eyes of the business owner. The lack of preparation for succession in Canada is reaching epic proportions, and this chapter is designed to help the business owner with some of the "big picture" issues, without going into too much technical detail.

INTRODUCTION

The Need for Planning

I n recent years, there has been no shortage of high-profile reports of significant, successful businesses running into succession problems. Family disagreements over control of Canadian Tire Corp. Ltd. and McCain Foods have highlighted the special problems surrounding family businesses. At the same time, business mergers and acquisitions seem to be increasing in size and frequency, with price tags that can strain our ability to comprehend large numbers.

As in all issues, however, reducing the business of a lifetime to a few short paragraphs can focus on only one or two of the salient facts. In the real world, the questions are never as clear, the answers are never as simple and the outcome is never as sure or predictable.

The Advantages of Planning

Yet many business owners today assume that, if their business has a value of, say, $2,000,000, then one day, when they decide it's time to retire, there will appear, as if from nowhere, a willing buyer. Indeed, a buyer who is not only willing, but who has the cash, the business expertise and the confidence to simply write the business owner a cheque and let him retire to a life of carving coconuts somewhere. In reality, it is likely that:

- The buyer will not have cash;
- The buyer will haggle over price;

- The buyer will want the seller to continue working for a period of months, even years; and

- From a tax point of view, whatever is advantageous for the buyer will work against the seller, and *vice versa*.

The entire process will be one compromise after another, on both sides, and all too often both the buyer and the seller will wonder if, somehow, they could have done better.

The key, of course, is to start the planning process sooner, long before a sale is even a remote possibility.

Consider the following examples:

Bill, approaching retirement at 60, has a wholesale florist business worth around $2,000,000. The business is incorporated, and shares are owned by Bill and his wife Joan on a $50/50$ basis. Over the years, Bill has encouraged his senior employees to become more and more involved in all management aspects of the business, in everything from bank financing to developing their new web page. Bill and Joan take frequent vacations and look forward to making them even more frequent. Long-established customers know that they can deal with the senior employees with complete confidence and do not have to keep to checking with Bill or Joan.

On the other side of town, Ben operates a similar business, with similar income and value. Ben has always owned 90% of the shares of the business, his wife Margaret owning the other 10%. In many ways, Ben has always been obsessed with control and perfection, and, naturally, has tended to do everything important himself, leaving his employees only the most routine tasks. Now, at the age of 60, Ben wants to retire. It will be nice to relax for a while — he and Margaret have not had a real vacation since the trip they won in a lottery seven years ago. That hadn't been much of a holiday anyway, as it was at a very busy time for the business and Ben had to phone the office several times a day to make sure no major problems came up.

With these fact patterns, it is clear that Bill's business will be much easier to sell than Ben's. In addition, Bill and Joan will keep more of their money, with less going to taxes (two small business gains exemptions). And, of course, the new owner will not have to rely as heavily on Bill and Joan's ongoing involvement, as the business is quite capable of managing without them.

The advantages of Bill and Joan's situation are not the result of last-minute re-organization to facilitate a sale, but rather of a long-term business approach with clearly established principles and objectives. It is this approach that makes Bill and Joan the exception rather than the rule.

The Succession Planning Team

So how did Bill and Joan get to this point? Evidently, they had good advisors, but, more importantly, they listened and participated in the process.

Who were these advisors? It is instructive to look at the different areas of expertise that could contribute to facilitating Bill and Joan's arrival at this point.

- Both Bill and Joan have clearly defined objectives, both financial and personal. These objectives were formulated by discussion, not just with each other, but also with their children and senior employees.

- While not yet financially independent without considering the value of the business, much pressure can be relieved if Bill and Joan have some kind of financial safety net, whether from an RRSP, a pension plan or an RCA. The ability to arrange a successful ownership transition is much greater if there is no "make or break" financial pressure;

- Ownership of the business on a $50/50$ basis provides the opportunity for significant tax saving, especially if the shares qualify for the Small Business Gains Exemption. Making sure that the shares qualify is an important ongoing responsibility;

- Involving key employees in the management process over the years facilitates an ownership transition with as few snags as possible. Assuming that Bill and Joan have no desire to give these key employees shares, the remuneration of these employees might include pension plans, profit-sharing plans, phantom stock plans and special bonus plans;

- Over the years, the key employees have developed a relationship with the company's banker, suppliers and major customers. If Bill and Joan are no longer involved, the business can continue without any major upheaval;

- When Bill and Joan sell the business, they will become investors of capital rather than employees/owners of a business. Significantly, they will feel some need to protect the capital as well as receive income — after retirement, they would see little opportunity to be able to rebuild lost capital;

- Transferring or selling the business to Bill and Joan's children was never an issue. This possibility was discussed and dismissed long ago. The children do not expect to inherit the business, nor do they expect to become rich as a result of the business. New owners will be able to run the business as it should be run;

- Financially, the business has always been sound. The relationship with lenders, suppliers and customers has been very strong;

- Financial statements, legal and tax filings are all up to date and all related information is readily accessible. All records and systems were computerized five years ago; and

- Personal investments were kept separate from the business whenever possible.

From the above, it is clear that the succession planning "team" will include all those same advisors who contributed to the success of the business and its owners in the first place:

1. Legal advisors,

2. Accounting advisors,

3. Investment advisors,

4. Insurance advisors,

5. Tax advisors, and

6. Bankers.

Whether this is two or three separate individuals or six, it is important that all of these disciplines be represented. The very factors that make the business a success will also make it saleable.

The Role of Tax Planning

It should be emphasized that tax planning is only one factor to be considered in the succession planning process. It would, for example, have been possible for Bill and Joan to minimize or even eliminate taxes altogether if they had arranged share ownership on an equal 25% basis with themselves and their two children. If their primary motivation was to avoid tax, then all well and good, but this is rarely the case — personal preferences and priorities usually take precedence. (Remember that 50% ownership would only give them 50% of the sale proceeds — the children would receive the other 50%.)

For this reason, it is important that the succession planning process be completed in the order of priority that is appropriate for the business owner:

1. What do I want to achieve?

2. What is the simplest and most direct way for me to achieve this?

3. What is the most tax-effective way for me to achieve this?

There are many examples of plans implemented to save taxes which in the long term proved to be counter-productive to the vendor, the purchaser and the families involved. It cannot be emphasized too strongly that the first and most important duty of the succession planning team is to help the business owner find out what he or she really wants. When the goal is clearly in sight, the mechanics of how to get there can readily be determined. Without a clear picture of the goal, the mechanics become irrelevant.

In the following chapters, we will examine some of the many pitfalls and opportunities surrounding the area of business succession planning, both for family-owned and non-family-owned businesses. In each instance, primary consideration will be given to the priorities and preferences of the owners. Tax saving will be seen as a way to assess various alternatives, rather than a reason in itself to embark upon a specific strategy.

Malcolm Scarratt
Bragg Creek, Alberta
August 2006

TABLE OF CONTENTS

Page

CHAPTER 1

Identifying a Buyer/Successor

P robably one of the most important tasks for any CEO or majority shareholder employee is to determine who would take over the business in the event of death, permanent disability or retirement. Sadly, it is a task that is often not planned, never enters into the current "To Do" list of most business owners, and is left to chance or to an assumption that some day, somehow, everything will work out just fine.

At this point, we are not primarily concerned with funding, just with trying to determine who would be best suited to take over. It sounds as if it should be a simple proposition, but it rarely is.

Many factors enter into a business owner's reluctance to take this essential step. While not a central theme of this book, we should pause long enough to identify some of these factors in the hope that being able to recognize them will help advisors to guide their clients through the process.

Typical reasons would include the following:

- The business owner's identity is so closely tied to the business itself that he or she MUST be involved (many business owners need help in seeing themselves and their businesses as two separate entities);

- The business owner is irreplaceable, and there's no point in looking for someone who could do everything he or she does;

- There will be lots of time for that sort of thing in the future, but right now there is a business to be run (sometimes, of course, there is NOT a lot of time, and everything collapses into chaos);

- With no obvious successor in sight, it is easier not to make a decision;

- Family dynamics can really complicate the issue (an issue discussed more fully in Chapter 5, "Family Owned Businesses");

- Successful businesses owners often believe that their businesses will be bought by some big conglomerate "in the next few years", so long-term planning is ignored;

- With no obvious solution to the problem of funding, why bother finding a successor?

In reality, it is prudent to identify a potential successor or successors and then be prepared to be flexible, since things always seem to change and rarely turn out the way we would expect.

Once a client makes the decision to embark upon the process of finding a buyer or successor, then there are just five general categories of prospects.

Other Shareholders

Other shareholders in the business are probably the most likely candidates, or at least they may seem to be. They know the business already and would often be willing to assume a larger share position. Usually, they are familiar with key suppliers and clients, as well as with bankers and other advisors.

Typically, however, there are other factors. If a business was started by its current shareholders, it is likely that they are fairly close in age. If a business was owned, for example, by two shareholders, one 57 and one 54, it is unlikely that the 54-year-old would be a prime candidate to take over the business when his or her fellow shareholder retires.

In addition, it is not uncommon for shareholders to have the great majority of their net worth tied up in the business. Personal investment capital can be hard to find and the idea of going into debt to buy more shares is not always attractive. In fact, many shareholders are already uncomfortable with so much of their net worth being in one place and may be more interested in diversification than in increasing their current shareholdings.

Many businesses already have Shareholders Agreements in place, specifying what happens when a shareholder dies or withdraws, and these will be examined in Chapter 7. These agreements routinely cover what happens in the event of the death of a shareholder, in the event of a dispute, in the event that a shareholder is permanently disabled, but they rarely address in detail how a shareholder will retire.

Employees

Many small businesses could logically be owned and continued by employees, who would often be happy to have the opportunity to take over. It is dangerous, however, to assume that this would always be the case. On many occasions, succession plans involving groups of employees have been designed only to have them fall apart at the last moment, when one or more employees realize that the financial risk is too great and that they are happier remaining employees rather than becoming owners.

It takes a special kind of employee to trade a regular paycheque and regular hours for the opportunity to go into debt, work longer hours, and have to pay everyone else first.

If a business owner sincerely wants an employee or group of employees to take over, then he or she has to be willing to be creative, and probably somewhat generous, when it comes to financing. It can be a successful transition, but it requires a lot of careful planning, done well in advance.

Competitors

In certain types of business, competitors may be a logical choice as future buyers. For example, two roofing contractors may be fierce competitors, controlling 80% of the local market. If one wants to retire, only the competitor would really understand the value of the business, so he or she would be a logical successor.

However, their status as competitors can easily impede discussions, since the sharing of information might be something neither is really willing to do, at least not until there are no other alternatives available.

Outsiders

Newspapers are commonly full of classified ads under "Businesses for sale", looking for individuals with capital to invest and with the ability to run a particular type of business. Many franchise operations are sold in this way, as are many retail stores.

It is difficult to sell a business as a "going concern", although it is possible for a suitable and qualified buyer to be found by this method.

Certain types of business may be attractive to investors with capital, but might not normally be businesses requiring "hands on" management, so the scope of opportunity here can be quite limited.

Family Members

The ideal solution for many business owners is to hand over the business to children. A true "family business" is a dream for many people and can provide a good solution to the problem of succession planning.

There are times, however, when such plans create many more problems than they solve. The normal family squabbles that take place in all families can be magnified many times over when a business is involved, especially when complicated by some of the toughest issues to overcome:

- When children marry, do the "outside" spouses have any share entitlement?

- What happens in the event of a divorce? and

- Should all children be treated equally, or is it sufficient for all to be treated fairly? Should shareholders working in the business have the same rights as shareholders who are simply passive investors?

On the positive side, the mutual support and commitment of family members can often succeed in solving business problems that would simply be too much for arm's length shareholders.

If there are five possible sources for future business owners, how does one decide where to look, and which is most appropriate? Of course, the details of the business and the specific personalities involved will sometimes make it obvious, but we can also draw some general conclusions:

- A company with older shareholders of approximately the same age will probably need to look beyond the shareholder group;

- A company with shareholders of widely differing ages may be able to organize succession planning within the group;

- Employee groups may consider share ownership if the process is made as painless as possible;

- Planning for transition in the event of death or disability can be dramatically different from planning for retirement;

- Businesses with significant trade secrets will find the process especially difficult;

- Businesses requiring the active involvement of the owner/manager in a specific skill area will not normally be attractive to outsiders;

- Involving an owner's children can cause resentment among employees if it is felt that the children have not earned their position. The children are often viewed more critically than any outsider would be, and may have to perform twice as well to appear half as good;

- Sale to a competitor is often seen as a last resort, and often there is simply insufficient trust for any meaningful dialogue;

- Businesses heavily dependent on the personality of an owner can be more difficult to sell than those dependent on a group of employees or a specific technology. These businesses generally require a much longer lead time to structure successor ownership; and

- The "white knight" bearing cash or a certified cheque for a full value purchase rarely appears. Creativity is the order of the day.

C H A P T E R

2

Selling at Retirement

S ociety's views on retirement have changed significantly over the years. In fact, they continue to evolve as technology and life-styles change. Consider the following views, all commonplace at some point in the last 20 years or so:

- Everyone retires at 65, ready or not;

7

- Earlier retirement is better;

- Increased wealth and more leisure opportunities mean that everyone will retire at 55;

- Working less or working differently is a better choice than retiring altogether;

- People with a reason to get up in the morning live longer; and

- With today's high taxes, retirement is becoming more difficult.

For the average employee, retirement is perhaps an easier proposition, or at least a more predictable one. Pension plans and Registered Retirement Savings Plans provide the necessary tax incentive to save for retirement. Interestingly, the recent reduction in maximum RRSP deferral age from 71 to 69 would indicate that many people actually can afford to defer as long as possible. For many people, the system works.

Consider the business owner. In the "survival" years, there was probably no money left for RRSP's or pensions. All available resources were devoted to the business. Eventually, the business begins to acquire real value; perhaps it will be a success after all. But it is still just numbers on paper. A net worth statement typically shows how little of the owner's worth is independent of the business.

As retirement age approaches, the business owner sees the opportunity to have a "payday", to see the numbers on paper transferred into cash in a bank account.

When reality sets in, it becomes apparent that the whole process will have to be one of accommodation and compromise. A disappointment, to put it mildly, but one which can be minimized with some advance planning in key areas.

Setting Objectives

Too often, we, as advisors, can be guilty of recommending solutions to problems the client has not really identified or may not even have. In the same way, business owner clients may find it all too easy to approach the question of retirement without really taking the time to ask themselves what they are really looking for.

Some years ago, one of the major banks ran an advertisement for RRSP's using the headline "Retirement is just not working", a clever attention-getter with multiple meanings. For the business owner, of course, retirement is a very complex process. Like a fine painting, it becomes more and more detailed as you get closer.

Before even considering how to retire, a business owner needs to define what retirement means to him or her, which will necessitate answering questions such as:

- Does he or she want capital or income? How much?

- Will the business continue to flourish and prosper without him or her?

- Is capital for children or grandchildren a consideration?

- Is there a charity or charities the owner would like to benefit, either now or in the future?

- Is finding the right buyer more important than getting the highest price?

- What will retirement look like? Is it the owner's intention to travel, to move offshore, to get into another business, to become an active investor, to write his or her memoirs, to write the great Canadian novel or to "hang out" with the grandchildren?

The answers will go a long way toward determining the style and structure of any buyout arrangement. In fact, the more time a client is willing to spend in determining objectives, the smoother and more certain the process becomes.

Getting Ready

It is entirely unreasonable for a business owner who has not taken a vacation in ten years to assume he or she can simply walk away from the business on retirement. Getting ready for retirement must include, as a practical matter, some sort of rehearsal or advance preparation. A business owner who takes a two-week vacation and phones the office twice a day is not ready for retirement, and is not providing his or her successor with the necessary "hands on" experience if no decision ever needs to be made without his or her input.

Most, if not all business owners believe the business could not function without them, but of course this is exactly contrary to the concept of retirement planning.

In part, this preparation consists of adopting a particular mind-set, but it is also a specific exercise to prepare the business for its independence from him or her. This involves grooming a successor, training employees to accept more responsibility, even preparing key customers to deal with the business in its new form.

Ideally, this process should begin well in advance of the proposed retirement date. There are always unforeseen obstacles, and starting early will allow time to discover them and make appropriate adjustments. It will also allow the owner to decide whether he or she really wants to retire, or whether some more gradual process would be better. In some businesses, one method of preparation is to give a potential successor total ownership of a specific project and then see how the project is handled. The project could be of short duration, say a week or two, or it could be a major project with a time frame of a year or more. The key is to hand over total ownership of the project, then avoid the temptation to keep checking on how things are going.

Sell Shares or Assets?

There is inevitably an element of conflict between the buyer and the seller in any transaction. Obviously, the buyer wants to pay the lowest price possible, and the seller wants to receive the highest price possible. In the sale of a business, the potential conflict is heightened by tax considerations. Different tax results will result from two basic alternatives:

(i) The business owner sells shares to the purchaser; or

(ii) The company sells its assets to the purchaser, pays appropriate corporate tax and distributes the remainder to the shareholder.

As a general rule, the vendor would normally prefer to sell shares and the purchaser would prefer to purchase assets, but of course this type of generalization has many exceptions, and the following are just some of the factors that need to be considered in order to determine the optimum approach:

- If the corporation is a qualified small business corporation (QSBC) then access to the small business gains exemption (SBGE) could provide up to $500,000 of capital gains on a tax-free basis. This will result in a strong preference for a sale of shares by the vendor;

- If shares are held by several family members, then the SBGE eligibility is even more attractive, assuming each shareholder can use the exemption;

- The amount of adjusted cost base in the vendor's shares might influence the choice, compared with the amount of adjusted cost base in the assets that would be sold by the corporation;

- Once the SBGE is used up, or if the shares do not qualify, then any capital gain will be taxed in the usual way, with a top rate of around 20%. The vendor would receive $800 after tax for every $1,000 of purchase price. The purchaser then has $1,000 of adjusted cost base.

If, on the other hand, the purchaser were to pay the vendor a $1,500 consulting fee, the vendor would net around $900 and the purchaser would have a net cost of around $825 if the fee were deductible at 45%. In this case, both the vendor and the purchaser would be better off.

Naturally, this type of arrangement has to pass the usual "reasonableness" test, and will not be appropriate in all situations, but it is an example of the kind of flexibility and creativity to be brought to the table in business purchase situations.

- The level of "safe income" in the business can also be a factor, as it would indicate how much tax-free dividend income might be available to the vendor via a holding company in the event that the company were to sell assets to the purchaser of the business;

- Similarly, a large amount of Refundable Dividend Tax on Hand (RDTOH) might give rise to an analysis of how efficiently money could be routed through the company rather than directly from the purchaser;

- Any Capital Dividend Account balance would normally be cleared first, but would again be an indicator in this type of analysis.

The above points are just a sample of the major factors to be considered and are meant to indicate that the choice is not necessarily a simple one. In most cases, specialized accounting advice would be a definite prerequisite once the question of shares or assets arises.

Walk Away or Stay Involved?

If a business has been built over the years largely by the special skills of the founding shareholder, then any buyer of that business would in all likelihood want the founder to stay on for a period of transition. This type of arrangement might last for up to two years, during which time the new owner could expect to see most kinds of normal business cycles and routines.

For many business owners, this is seen as a period of freedom during which they can act on a consulting basis without worrying about the finances of the business (assuming they are paid out, which is not always the case, of course).

If this arrangement is contemplated, then it is essential for each of the parties to agree on what is expected, for how long, how often, under what circumstances and for what remuneration. Is it to be related to profits or some performance criteria, or is it simply a guarantee for a period of time?

There will be times when a consulting contract can be an integral part of the sale process, but there are others when it would be a disaster. This will depend in large part on the personalities involved. If it does not work well, then the former owner and the new owner will quickly come to resent each other's presence. The advisors who participate in structuring the sale must know the personalities of the clients, which further emphasizes the importance of the "getting ready" phase.

There are few possible permutations at work here. Should the vendor stay involved after the sale?

1. Vendor says yes. Purchaser says no.

2. Vendor says yes. Purchaser says yes.

3. Vendor says no. Purchaser says no.

4. Vendor says no. Purchaser says yes.

Situations two and three do not present a problem, since the parties agree.

Situations one and four would probably be worked out in terms of income or purchase price or a combination of the two. For example, in situation one, the vendor might offer to take a lower sale price in favour of having a salary and staying involved. In situation four, the purchaser could increase his or her offering price in order to induce the vendor to stay involved, or could make the salary offer very attractive. Salary payments should be deductible, so the purchaser might prefer that route.

For the vendor who is not really ready to retire, a consulting contract can be an ideal transition vehicle, but, when all is said and done, it often comes down to money.

Financing

In an ideal world, buyer and seller would agree on a price, the buyer would write the seller a cheque and the two would go their separate ways to live happily ever after.

In reality, it is usually the creativity of financing that determines whether the deal can be done. As was mentioned earlier, the process often becomes one of accommodation and compromise.

For the purpose of this section, we will use the following hypothetical situation:

- Vendor: Mr. V, age 60, owns 100% of VCo;
- Purchaser: Mr. P, age 45;
- Business Value: $1,000,000;
- ACB of shares: $0;
- VCo is a QSBC*;
- Mr. V has not used any SBGE;
- Mr. V has a top marginal tax rate of 40%.

* A Qualified Small Business Corporation is a Canadian-Controlled Private Corporation in which all or substantially all (assumed to be 90%) of the assets are used to earn income in an active business. In addition, at least 50% of the assets must have been used to earn active business income at all times during the preceding 24 months. The shares of a QSBC are eligible for the Small Business Gains Exemption of $500,000 if the shares have been held by the individual in question (or by someone that individual doesn't deal with at arm's length) for a period of at least 24 months.

Using this data, we can analyze various alternatives:

Cash

- Mr. P writes Mr. V a cheque for $1,000,000;
- Mr. P now has a $1,000,000 ACB for the shares of VCo;
- Mr. V receives $1,000,000, realizing a capital gain of $1,000,000;
- Mr. V claims $500,000 Small Business Gains Exemption, leaving $500,000 of gain; resulting in tax payable of $100,000.

Mr. V walks away with $900,000 net after tax. If he can earn an 8% rate of return, he would have an annual pre-tax income of $72,000 without touching capital.

Bank Loan

- Mr. P borrows $1,000,000 from his bank, then writes Mr. V a cheque for $1,000,000;

- Mr. V's position is the same as in "Cash" section above;

- Mr. P now has to repay the bank. At 6%, he would make annual payments of $136,000 for 10 years.

Over the 10 years, this will take $1,360,000 to repay. If interest is deductible and principal is non-deductible, then this will require:

- $2,027,000 of pre-tax personal earnings if taxed at 40%; or

- $1,610,000 of pre-tax corporate earnings if taxed at 20% in a corporation.

So, on average, it would require between $161,000 and $202,700 of earnings each year to retire the debt.

Would the business itself support this? If not, then Mr. P would want to re-think the purchase price.

Vendor Financing

If Mr. V is willing to provide the financing, then he could effectively put himself in the same position as the bank in the previous example. Mr. P's position is unchanged, but Mr. V, in becoming banker as well as vendor, changes his view of things quite dramatically.

Mr. V will receive $136,000 annually for 10 years, assuming the same 6% interest. In the early years, most of the payment would be taxed as interest income:

Years	Interest	Principal
1	60,000	76,000
2	55,448	80,420
3	50,623	85,245
4	45,508	90,360
5	40,086	95,782
6	34,340	101,528
7	28,248	107,620

Years	Interest	Principal
8	21,791	114,077
9	14,946	120,922
10	7,690	128,177

The early years would be particularly difficult, as Mr. V would also have to include in income 20% of the capital gain each year for five years, so, from a cash flow position, the first five years would look as follows:

Year	Interest Income	Capital Gain	SBGE available	Total taxable	Tax at 40%
1	80,000	200,000	100,000	130,000	52,000
2	74,478	200,000	100,000	124,418	49,791
3	68,513	200,000	100,000	118,513	47,405
4	62,072	200,000	1,000	112,000	44,800
5	55,116	200,000	10,000	105,116	42,046

Mr. V's after-tax cash flow in this example is dramatically reduced, and his investment alternatives are effectively postponed. This would be a difficult arrangement for Mr. V to accept financially.

Even worse, his cash flow stream would still be at risk. If the business were to encounter financial difficulties, whether due to an overall economic downturn or to some level of incompetence on the part of Mr. P, then there would be a very real possibility of payments going into default. Depending on Mr. P's other resources, Mr. V may have little recourse other than to take back the shares, which of course will, under these circumstances, have little value.

It is clear that this type of arrangement would not be at the top of Mr. V's priority list. Rather than $1,000,000 financed over 10 years, he might settle for a lesser amount if paid in cash, or a combination of cash and financing. If he has a clear picture of his objectives, then he is, of course, much better equipped to make this kind of evaluation.

Reducing Business Value

If Mr. V is at the point where he is about to retire, then much of his attention may be devoted to sources of retirement income, rather than sources of capital. If this is the case, then it may be possible for him to reduce business value by having VCo set up a Retirement Compensation Arrangement (RCA) for him, or an Individual Pension Plan (IPP) or pay him a retiring allowance to allow him to supplement his RRSP funds.

Technically, this approach is not a buyout mechanism, and the details of structuring and funding an RCA or IPP are beyond the scope of our current analysis, but it is important to bear in mind the principle involved. This type of pension funding would have a twofold advantage:

- It would reduce the value of VCo and thereby make the purchase easier;

- It would provide Mr. V with an income source not dependent on the ongoing viability of VCo.

Shifting From Capital to Income

As long as Mr. V is determined to have capital, he is faced with these financing obstacles. If he could somehow come to terms with leaving the capital where it is for now (invested in VCo) then he would be able to examine some other alternatives. This will depend on who the buyer is, and is perhaps easier in a non-arm's length sale where there may be a greater element of trust.

Looking back to the "ideal" of a cash purchase, Mr. V would receive $900,000 after tax and could expect an annual income (pre-tax) of $72,000, if earnings averaged 8% annually. If this income were taxed at an average 27% (a mix of interest, dividends and capital gain), Mr. V would earn around $52,560 after tax.

Suppose Mr. V and Mr. P were to come to the following arrangement:

- Mr. V exchanges all his common shares in VCo for redeemable, retractable preferred shares (at $1,000,000 value);

- VCo issues new common shares (at $0 value) to Mr. P;

- VCo will pay a dividend of $80,000 on the preferred shares owned by Mr. V;

- VCo will insure the life of Mr. V for $1,000,000 to fund the redemption of the preferred shares on his death.

Like all possible arrangements, this has its advantages and disadvantages.

Advantages:

- $80,000 of dividend income would net Mr. V as much as $60,000 if taxed at 25%;

- Mr. V's estate will ultimately receive $1,000,000, most or all of which could be tax-free (see Chapter 4, "Sale on Death");

- Mr. P does not borrow $1,000,000 to fund the purchase; and

- Less pressure on corporate cash flow will benefit VCo and increase its chance of survival.

Disadvantages:

- Dividend income to Mr. V must be paid from after-tax income of VCo;

- Mr. V is still dependent on viability of VCo;

- VCo would have to pay life insurance costs of around $20,000 annually; and

- Mr. V never has capital to invest elsewhere.

Discussion Points:

- Life insurance costs could be reduced by insuring Mr. V and Mrs. V on a joint life second-to-die basis, as long as it is acceptable to have the shares redeemed on the second death;

- Mr. V would want some form of security, if at all possible; and

- Mr. V would also want his preferred shares to have voting control, perhaps structured in such a way as to gradually cede control to Mr. P over a period of time.

In many instances, it is likely that several financing options will be used at once. Even in situations where one option seems to be the obvious answer, it is helpful for the advisor to at least review whatever other options may be available. In this way, buyer and seller can arrive at an agreement that is custom-made and addresses the objectives of both of them. Indeed, one way of recognizing the ideal solution is if both parties think that they "did OK" in the negotiations but could perhaps have done a little better. It is essential for the parties to recognize the "win/win" nature of the process, and this can only be achieved if all alternatives are at least considered, even if not examined in detail.

Tax Planning

Once the decision to sell has been made, and the owner decides to consider retirement, then an analysis of the tax status of the vendor, the purchaser and the company becomes essential.

Assuming the corporation is a Qualified Small Business Corporation, then we can consider the Small Business Gains Exemption. If the SBGE is available, then the vendor will want to trigger capital gains of at least that much. The SBGE will not be used if the company sells assets, nor if it redeems shares.

If the SBGE is not available, either because the company is not a QSBC or because the vendor has already used the SBGE elsewhere, then a capital gains transaction would still benefit the vendor, since dividends are taxed at a slightly higher rate than capital gains (currently around 25%, compared with 20% for capital gains). Note that this preference may change from province to province, depending on marginal tax rates.

If the vendor had been able to introduce other family members as shareholders, then there is the possibility of multiple eligibility for the SBGE. This argues in favour of tax planning well in advance of a share disposition (see Chapter 6, Small Business Gains Exemption).

The Transition from Business Owner to Investor of Capital

When a business owner successfully negotiates the sale of a business as a going concern, it is often the first time in that owner's lifetime that he or she has ever had a significant amount of capital. This can be both exciting and intimidating.

Instead of going to work and earning money by providing goods or services in which he has some real expertise, the retired owner will earn money by investing capital, likely an activity in which he or she has no particular experience or expertise. This often gives rise to a conflict that is difficult to resolve, and here the role of the financial advisor changes significantly.

In the process of retirement, the vendor will expect to invest conservatively. In the earlier example, Mr. V sold VCo for $1,000,000 and had $900,000 (after tax) available for investment. If he were to invest in term deposits at 5%, his pre-tax income would be $45,000 and it would be fully taxable at regular rates. This is a disappointing return on a lifetime's work, and indeed may be insufficient for Mr. V to live on. Before retirement, he was an owner of a million-dollar business and had a salary of $150,000. Now, even after a cash sale for full value, he has an investment fund of $900,000 and an income of $45,000

Initially, Mr. V will be reluctant to use up any capital and will want to minimize risk. The role of his advisors will be to arrange the investment fund in such a way as to minimize risk, minimize tax and maximize income — a difficult combination, but one which is attainable over a period of time once the retired owner has accurately assessed the concept of risk and its relative importance.

In the early months, perhaps even years, liquidity and flexibility will be important to facilitate changes in investment philosophy, and investments will likely be short-term in nature. It is crucial for the retired business owner to appreciate this period of adjustment and not to panic or make question-able decisions.

In this respect, a period of consulting for the new owner can be very helpful in smoothing over the adjustment from a financial point of view.

As advisors, we should not assume that the business owner can become an astute and confident investor simply by virtue of having cash to invest, and our role here is a continuation of the consulting process begun before the sale was contemplated.

Retaining Key Employees

Whenever ownership of a business changes, continuity in day-to-day opera-tions and customer contact has to come from employees. In many cases, key employees are vital to the success of the ownership transition.

While a detailed examination of employee incentive techniques is beyond our current scope, it is important to have some awareness of the alternatives available.

In a competitive business environment, employee benefits such as group insurance coverages and group RRSP's are commonly expected and not always particularly appreciated.

There is a psychological difference between a pension plan and an RRSP, however. The pension plan conveys the concept of long service, of a retirement funded by the employer, whereas an RRSP is, thanks in large measure to the annual advertising blitz, a tax-shelter opportunity. The pension plan has more onerous reporting requirements and involves more effort on the employer's part, but does convey a different message.

Benefit plans can also be "custom tailored" for senior or key employees by the use of some of the new generation of Universal Life insurance, disability insurance, critical illness insurance and long-term care insurance policies. Creative plan design is the order of the day and is, in many instances, the crucial component of a plan, of significantly greater importance than trying to find the lowest costs available.

In some companies, it is evident that one or two key employees are the real "drivers" of the business, possessing superior sales skills or technical knowledge. These employees may be a target for competitors. The new owner of such a business would be vitally interested in having them stay, and may be willing to provide them with some form of equity position in the company. Typically, even senior employees have limited investment capital and little entrepreneurial drive, so trying to sell shares to them at fair market value might not be an attractive proposition. There are, however, several viable alternatives:

(i) A stock option plan, providing key employees the right to acquire shares at certain future times at a price determined in advance. Section 7 of the *Income Tax Act* provides some advantages if this type of plan meets certain criteria. If, for example, an employee has an option to buy shares for $10 (and the share value is not more than $10 when the option is granted), when the option is exercised he can purchase shares for $10 regardless of the market value. If market value is $15 when the option is exercised, the $5 advantage is not taxed immediately, but 50% of it is taxed as employment income when the shares are subsequently disposed of. Any growth beyond $15 would be taxed as capital gain in the usual way. The advantage of this approach is that it allows employees to buy in at a discount if share value increases.

A significant disadvantage is that the employees actually become shareholders, acquiring the rights of minority shareholders. This may not sit well with the new owner.

(ii) The new owner could instead institute an Employee Profit Sharing Plan, in which employees simply receive income each year based on some reference to profits. (section 144 of the *Income Tax Act*) If, for example, a business had pre-tax profits of $400,000, it could provide that any profits in excess of the $400,000 would be paid to all employees or a group of employees, either in whole or in part.

In this way, employees would derive tangible benefit from business increases.

Advantages of an EPSP include the fact that no registration with the Canada Revenue Agency is necessary, no actual share ownership is involved and the limits are subject only to the willingness of the business owner.

Disadvantages centre around the lack of tax-sheltering available. Amounts allocated annually to employees are fully taxable in the year of allocation and are taxed as employment income.

(iii) A "phantom stock plan" or Share Appreciation Rights Plan, provides a combination of (i) and (ii) and can be an effective long-term incentive plan. As an example, suppose Mr. P buys VCo from Mr. V for $1,000,000. We would assume that VCo was worth $1,000,000. Mr. P, the new owner, meets with two key employees, both of whom are 50 years old, and agrees to pay each of them, if they remain with VCo to age 60, 5% of the growth in value of VCo from today until that time.

If VCo was worth $2,000,000 in 10 years' time, then each of the employees would be entitled to 5% of the $1,000,000 of growth, or $50,000.

If either employee leaves VCo prior to age 60, that entitlement is forfeited. This approach requires a clear understanding on everyone's part as to how VCo will be valued. The $50,000 amount above would be taxed as employment income, but no taxable amounts are reported in the intervening ten years as long as the employees have no entitlement during that time.

Again, a major advantage from the owner's point of view is that no actual share ownership is involved. While the amounts are fully taxable as income, they should be deductible to VCo, so the tax treatment seems reasonable, especially if income tax rates continue to decline, as they have in the past few years.

Without this kind of thinking on Mr. P's part, the risk of key employees leaving VCo may be one not worth taking. His $1,000,000 investment could all too easily be in jeopardy if he simply works on the assumption that all employees will stay regardless of whether or not he makes any special arrangements.

In this process of the sale of VCo, part of the role of the advisor must include ensuring that the employees have the will and the incentive to stay.

C H A P T E R

3

Sale on Disability

D isability is one of the most difficult problems to deal with, both from the shareholder's point of view and from the business's point of view. In many businesses, it is a problem that is overlooked or ignored. A key function for any advisor is to ensure that it is discussed and considered, even if no "tidy" solution is identified, the discussion itself can be a useful exercise.

Defining the Problem

In many ways, a total and permanent disability can be as devastating to a business and to a business owner as can a premature death. It raises the same issues relating to survival of the business, maintenance of customer relationships and income for the owner's family, but has the added dimension of income for the owner himself.

In discussing the issue of disability, it is crucial that the advisor address with the business owner the following issues:

- Will the business continue to function in the event of a total disability?

- Where will the owner find income?

- If the disability is short-term, who will keep things running?

- If the disability is permanent, who will take over?

In Chapter 2, we looked at the issue of retirement. Usually, retirement at least allows some time for planning. Disability presents many of the same issues as retirement, but provides none of the time for planning.

Statistically, a long-term or permanent disability is several times more likely than death prior to retirement age, yet life insurance planning almost invariably receives considerably more attention, probably because life insurance issues are easier to solve. The injection of large amounts of tax-free cash into a business by way of life insurance proceeds can go a long way towards solving a great many problems, while disability insurance proceeds have less flexibility and fewer tax preferences.

It is not uncommon to find classified advertisements headed "for sale due to illness", and potential buyers are often looking for "fire sale" prices.

The list of potential buyers is the same list as in the sale on retirement: family members, employees, competitors and other shareholders. The structure and the process become significantly different, however, in the event of a disability.

Alternative Solutions and Financing

As an example, consider the firm of AB Ltd.

Shareholders:

- A, age 50: 50%;

- B, age 40: 50%;

- Value: $2,000,000;

- ACB: 0;

- PUCV: 0;

A becomes disabled. It looks as if he will not return to work, but that is not yet a certainty.

At what point does B have to act? Does A's salary continue for three months? Six months? A year or more? Eventually, B will probably decide to buy A's shares.

Purchase by B

After 12 months, B offers to buy A's shares for $1,000,000. B has no cash of course, and agrees to pay A over a five-year period. With no funding in place, A reluctantly agrees that the payments can be made without interest. So A will receive $200,000 annually, paid at the rate of $16,667 monthly. Assuming the shares qualify for the SBGE, $500,000 will be received by A tax-free. The balance will trigger tax of around $100,000, leaving A with $900,000 to invest for income.

AB Ltd. is now owned 100% by B, and B's shares have an ACB of $1,000,000. In order to pay A, B has had to earn up to an extra $333,333 annually. Capital payments to A have to made out of after-tax income. If AB Ltd. is worth $2,000,000, can it support this level of income to B? It has no ongoing salary payments to A, admittedly, but paying B an extra $333,333 would certainly create a problem of some sort.

Purchase by AB Ltd.

Instead of using his own money and having to take extra taxable income, B could have AB Ltd. purchase the shares owned by A.

This would change the nature of the transaction in several ways:

- When AB Ltd. buys back A's shares, payments are not treated as capital, but as an income transaction. Section 84(3) of the Act provides that any amount paid by AB Ltd. in excess of the paid-up capital value of the shares is deemed to be a dividend. In this example, paid-up capital value of the shares is $0, which keep the numbers neat, but in reality, there is likely to be a nominal paid-up capital of $100 or so, usually representing the original subscription price of the shares when the corporation came into existence;

- Since A receives dividend income, there is no eligibility for the Small Business Gains Exemption. In this example, the full amount received will be taxable as a dividend;

- If AB Ltd. has the cash, it can pay A for his shares without the cash having to go through another tax cycle in B's hands as was the case in the "Purchase by B" section above, so this method appears to have some tax efficiency;

- If AB Ltd. has to borrow the cash, the apparent tax efficiency is lost, since the company will have to repay the loan using after-tax income; and

- The tax efficiency was really an illusion anyway, since B, who considers himself the real purchaser, even though the company foots the bill, acquires no increase in adjusted cost base. In effect, the gain that has been taxed in A's hands as a dividend will be taxed again as capital gain when B eventually dies or disposes of his shares.

Although this method seems to have some advantages, primarily ones of simplicity and the avoidance of an extra tax bill for B, it can result in the worst of all possible worlds.

	B purchases	AB Ltd. purchases
Purchase Price	$1,000,000	$1,000,000
Capital Gains Exemption	500,000	0
Taxable to A	250,000	1,000,000
Tax paid by A	100,000	250,000
Net cash to A	900,000	750,000
ACB increase to B	1,000,000	0

Freeze and Redeem

In defining the problem of disability, A and B, prior to A's disability and in conjunction with their financial advisors, should agree on what the essential components of a disability buyout plan should be.

In most instances, it will be agreed that the major requirement of the disabled shareholder is income, not capital. The major requirements of the non-disabled shareholder will be survival of the company and equitable treatment of his disabled shareholder.

It may even be possible that A will recover and want to return to work.

A strategy that may well accommodate all of these considerations is the "freeze and redeem" approach:

- Immediately upon long-term disability (after a period of time mutually agreed upon in advance) A and B agree to a corporate reorganization under section 86 of the Act. Following the reorganization, A owns redeemable and retractable preferred shares with a value of $1,000,000 and an adjusted cost base of $0 or $500,000 (depending on the desire to use the SBGE); B owns common shares with a fair market value of $1,000,000 and an ACB of $0 or $500,000 (again, depending on SBGE utilization);

- Since A's interest in AB Ltd. is fixed in value, any increase in the value of AB Ltd. will accrue to the common shares owned by B;

- A receives annual dividend income on his preferred shares;

- Shares owned by A are redeemed from his estate on A's death (see Chapter 4, "Sale on Death"); and

- Voting rights would be negotiated in the planning process. Ideally, A would want to have voting rights attached to his shares, but this would be less appropriate as time passes.

This approach leaves A's capital tied up in AB Ltd., so it may not be an acceptable solution in all cases. It should at least, however, be considered if it meets most of the objectives of both parties. Just as in a sale on retirement, creativity is the order of the day.

If A had sold to B, he would have netted $900,000, which, at an 8% yield, would provide pre-tax income of $72,000. In the "freeze and redeem" scenario, AB Ltd. could pay a dividend of $60,000 to A, taxed at 25% (in Alberta), which would put him in an equal or better position.

If A were to recover and want to return to work at AB Ltd., a further share re-organization could be carried out to restore A to a common share position (not necessarily 50:50 with B, since the value of AB Ltd. may have increased in the period since A became disabled).

This is not a perfect solution. Neither is it an easy solution to negotiate and document, but it has several advantages over the normal "wait and see" approach that seems to prevail all too often.

Disability Insurance

Disability insurance is an essential component of any plan to purchase shares in the event of a shareholder's disability. There are primarily two kinds of disability insurance:

(i) Disability Income Insurance, to provide income during a period of disability; and

(ii) Disability Buyout Insurance, to provide cash to fund a commitment to purchase shares in the event of disability.

Disability Income Insurance

As a rule, disability income insurance provides for a payment of a monthly income after an elimination period (to avoid small claims for illnesses such as flu or the common cold) of 30 to 120 days. The longer the elimination period (and therefore the more small claims are avoided) the lower the cost.

A crucial consideration is the way in which disability is defined in the contract or policy. The definition of disability can range from "inability to perform any work for remuneration or profit" to "inability to perform the duties of his or her regular occupation at the time he or she became disabled", and of course the cost will vary in accordance with the definition as well as with the elimination period.

In the example of AB Ltd., the company could insure A for a monthly income sufficient for them to pay him an income of $60,000 annually, or $5,000 monthly.

When A becomes disabled, AB Ltd. receives $5,000 monthly, tax-free, and can pay this as a dividend on A's preferred shares. If this income stream started after 90 days, then AB Ltd. would agree to continue A's salary for the first 90 days.

During this time, the value of A's interest in AB Ltd. is frozen at $1,000,000. If the value of AB Ltd. increases, it will presumably be through the efforts of B rather than A, so B's shares will increase in value accordingly.

The disability income paid to AB Ltd. by the insurance policy would typically continue to A's age 65, at which time benefits would cease (some policies provide benefits for life in the event of a disability resulting from an accident rather than an illness).

At that time, B could start to purchase shares from A. Alternately, AB Ltd. could start to redeem shares over a period of time, or continue to pay the $60,000 to A regardless of the insurance funding running out.

Disability Buy-Sell Insurance

The second type of disability insurance normally has a longer elimination period. A buyout of shares is not normally triggered until after one year, sometimes two years, of continuous and total disability. If, for example, B or AB Ltd. agrees to buy A's shares for $1,000,000, then a disability buy-sell insurance policy might typically provide funding of $500,000 on a lump sum basis, with monthly payments to provide the balance. Unlike disability income insurance, disability buy-sell coverage is structured on a reimbursement basis, and coverage from the policy will be tailored to reflect actual payments made to the disabled shareholder. A $1,000,000 purchase price could be structured as $500,000 cash, paid after a one year waiting period, followed by 60 monthly payments of $8,333.

Disability benefits would be paid to B or AB Ltd., whoever was to be the purchaser of A's shares, and the same purchaser would also be the owner and premium payor of the policy.

Benefits received by B or AB Ltd. from a disability buy-sell policy will be received tax-free, as disability insurance benefits. Payments made to A, the disabled shareholder, will of course be payments for shares and will be taxed accordingly. The only way for A to receive tax-free income in the event of disability would be for him to arrange personal disability coverage or group disability coverage (assuming premiums were paid by him or charged to him) and, of course, this would then be completely separate from the buyout of his shares.

Disability buyout coverage for a healthy 50-year old male non-smoker would cost in the neighbourhood of $650 monthly, so this type of coverage is not particularly inexpensive. In our AB Ltd. example, $650 monthly is of course a good "trade-off" for the $1,000,000 purchase price of A's shares, but it would only be available if AB Ltd. had already purchased the coverage.

Insurance coverage always has to be purchased at a time when it is not needed if it is to be available when it is needed. It is clear that $650 monthly is less than $1,000,000 (representing about 0.75% of the capital amount) but it should be remembered that $650 monthly is a certainty (it will be paid) whereas the $1,000,000 benefit is a possibility (it will only be paid in the event that A becomes disabled during the currency of this disability policy).

Adjudication

In a closely held corporation, shareholders are typically friends as well as co-workers. The relationship is far more than one of business and contracts.

In this environment, the disability of a shareholder can be traumatic for both partners. While some disabilities are self-evident (heart-attack, automobile accident) there are many others that can appear relatively subjective (depression, stress, anxiety, back pain and other soft-tissue injuries and the general class of mental and nervous disorders).

This makes a disability buy-out particularly troublesome. Who will make the determination that a shareholder is actually disabled? Suppose A and B have been shareholders together for 20 years. A claims to be unable to work because of some "invisible" disability, although he still drops in to the office a couple of times a week "just to see how things are going". Is it easier for A and B to discuss whether A is really disabled, and whether A's shares should be "frozen" or purchased, or would it be better if some independent third party with specific expertise in this area were to make that decision?

This non-financial consideration can be one of the strongest motivators to fund a disability share purchase agreement with disability insurance, whether disability income or disability buy-sell coverage. The insurance company then assumes responsibility for determining whether a shareholder is disabled or not. For these purposes, there is no requirement for full funding. AB Ltd., for example, could insure A and B for, say, $100,000 of lump sum funding. In the event of a disability, the insurer will determine whether or not a shareholder is disabled and the share purchase can take place, using the $100,000 of funding as a down payment.

This type of funding could be put in place on A and B for a total of about $1,500 annually. It would avoid a source of potential conflict between shareholders at the worst possible time, and it would "jump start" the buyout process. It is not a substitute for full funding, but can play a vital part in the planning process.

Tax Planning

For a sale on disability, the same basic tax planning considerations exist as for selling at retirement.

If the Small Business Gains Exemption is available, then the disabled shareholder will want to receive capital gains to take advantage of the exemption. Once the exemption is used up, then his or her preference will vary according to the tax treatment of capital gains and dividends in his or her province of residence. In our example, capital gains are taxed at an effective 20% and dividends at 25%. The purchaser will normally continue to prefer a capital transaction, which would provide him/her with an increase in adjusted cost base.

When we look at dividends being paid to a 50% shareholder, we should also consider the use of a holding company:

If A, the disabled shareholder in our example, transfers his AB Ltd. shares to Holdco A (a tax-deferred "rollover" under section 85 of the *Income Tax Act*), the dividends paid to Holdco A by AB Ltd. could pass to Holdco A tax-free, subject to AB Ltd. having sufficient "safe income" (after-tax retained earnings) and to Holdco A having more than 10% of the votes and value in AB Ltd.

Suppose that AB Ltd. were to pay $60,000 of dividend to Holdco A. This amount could be received tax-free by Holdco A, but has no real advantage if A then has to declare a dividend to himself from Holdco A. If, on the other hand, A can afford to leave the dividend in Holdco A (having looked after income requirements by the use of disability insurance, for example), then he can accumulate funds for investment in Holdco A without triggering tax other than on the investment income earned by those funds. This can be a significant advantage to A.

In this type of arrangement, care should be taken to ensure that subsection 55(2) of the *Income Tax Act* does not apply. Subsection 55(2) is designed to prevent what would be a taxable capital gain from being converted into a tax-free intercorporate dividend. It would not apply if AB Ltd. were simply paying dividend income to Holdco A its shares in AB Ltd., or if AB Ltd has sufficient "safe income", but it might well apply if AB Ltd. were to begin a program of repurchasing its shares held by Holdco A. A detailed analysis of subsection 55(2) is not appropriate here, but advisors do need to be aware of its impact and applicability and to at least recognize situations in which it may be a factor.

Tax planning for a sale triggered by the disability of a shareholder depends in large part on the planning done by the corporation and shareholders over the years:

- Do shares qualify for the SBGE, or has the SBGE already been converted to ACB?

- Are holding companies in place?

- Is disability insurance in place?

- Are other family members involved in the holding companies?

- Does a disabled shareholder need income or capital?

In theory, these issues should be less problematic as a shareholder gets closer to retirement age. By that time, some kind of succession plan should be in place, and disability insurance will normally terminate at retirement or at a specific age. (It should be noted that disability insurance covers "earned income" only and is typically restricted to the years prior to retirement.)

CHAPTER 4

Sale on Death

I n many corporations, even those where no real planning has been done, no successors identified, and no contingency plans are in place, the corporation still owns life insurance on its major shareholders. Whilst this is at least one responsible course of action, it is indicative of a major problem in the area of succession planning in the event of the death of a major shareholder. The belief does exist that all one has to do in order to solve issues related to death is buy a sufficiently large life insurance policy. The ready availability and relative inexpensiveness of life insurance can push other important planning issues into the background and create a false sense of security.

As someone who has worked in the life insurance industry ever since leaving university, I would be the last person to downplay the advantages of life insurance, but it is best used when it complements, rather than replaces, the other components of succession planning. Admittedly, life insurance plus no planning is usually a better combination than planning plus no life insurance, since tax-free cash does have its way of solving a multitude of problems.

Setting Objectives

Many business owners postpone succession planning not because it is not important, and not because of its potential expense but because, faced with their own mortality, they simply do not know what to do. The raw nerves exposed in the succession planning process can unsettle even the most calculating business owner. If he or she can somehow sidetrack the discussion and concentrate on some issue such as the relative merits of different kinds of life insurance, then maybe that is an acceptable trade-off for him or her.

The advisor's primary function in this area is not so much the resolution of problems, but rather the discovery of problems. Just to keep things interesting, the problems will change as time progresses, so we must constantly check to see that planning done so far is still appropriate.

As an example, consider the following case study:

- Acme Widgets Inc. was founded 20 years ago by Bill and Ben. Bill, who owns 75% of the business, is 40 years old. Ben, who is 38, owns the remaining 25% of the company;

- Bill's son, Junior, is 21 and has just enrolled in a four-year Commerce degree (following two years of "finding himself" in the South Pacific);

- Bill's daughter, Lisa, is 18 and just completing high school;

- Ben's son, Alec, is seven; and

- Neither Bill's wife, Kelly, nor Ben's wife, Laura, have been involved in the business.

Up to the current time, it would be prudent for Bill and Ben to have a shareholder agreement (see Chapter 7) specifying that in the event of the death of either of them, the survivor would become the sole shareholder, whether by share purchase by the survivor or by share repurchase by Acme Widgets Inc.

Bill's primary concerns to this date would be that, in the event of his death, his family would be financially secure and that Acme Widgets Inc. would survive without too much disruption.

On Bill's death, Ben's major concerns would be that Bill's family should not become directly involved, and of course that the business should survive.

But as time passes, Bill's objectives are changing, and a new set of considerations begins to pre-occupy Bill:

- Eventually, he would like Junior to come into the business and become a shareholder;

- He wants to treat Lisa fairly and not to discriminate too blatantly in Junior's favour; and

- If he wants his share of the business to go to Junior (or Junior and Lisa), then he needs to make other arrangements for the financial independence of his wife in the event of his death, since the value of the business will not be available to her.

Clearly, the shareholder agreement between Bill and Ben will soon need to be revised. Meanwhile, the two shareholders need to discuss the upcoming changes and to agree on a degree of flexibility. The point here is that the planning process is not something to be done and put away.

It is too easy to assume that planning for a sale on death simply requires a shareholder agreement. The real issues requiring consideration as objectives will be:

- Who will run the company?

- Who should buy shares?

- Who should sell (maybe not just the deceased shareholder's estate)?

- How will the children be treated?

- How will taxes be paid?

- Should bank indebtedness be insured?

- What role will be played by key employees?

- Is it acceptable for the family of the deceased to be financially dependent in any way on the company, or is a clean break mandatory? This will, of course, have a major impact on financing.

- Apart from a requirement for cash to pay the purchase price for the shares, will the death of a shareholder result in any other needs for cash?

- If any tax advantages are available in the course of a share purchase or share repurchase, should these advantages go to surviving shareholders, or to the estate or family of the deceased shareholder?

Interim vs. Long-Term Solutions

Once objectives are determined, then it will be easy to decide whether the required solutions should be short-term or long-term.

Returning to the Acme Widgets Inc. example above, the short-term solution was for Bill and Ben to agree to buy each other's shares in the event of death. This would be appropriate until it becomes likely that either of Bill's children will enter the business. Note that it is possible for a short-term or interim solution to be in place for 20 years or more, so it is not what one would normally think of as short-term.

If shareholders have an agreement calling for a share purchase to take place at age 60, for example, then would it be appropriate to buy a long-term funding solution, such as permanent life insurance? Temporary coverage to age 60 would seem to be adequate, unless the insurance coverage is designed as an integral part of the retirement buyout solution. The various types of buyout cannot be isolated and each must ultimately be in balance with the others. Ideally, funding mechanisms and vehicles should be flexible enough to accommodate changing scenarios.

One common concern is that problems and solutions may be mismatched, teaming a long-term solution with a short-term problem or *vice-versa*. Again, a primary function of the advisor is to make sure that this mismatching is minimized, and that the clients are aware of any mismatch that will require further action in the future.

Cross Purchase vs. Corporate Share Repurchase

A fundamental question regarding a purchase of shares on death is whether the corporation should buy back its own shares or whether the buyer should be an individual or individuals.

Tax outcomes vary significantly according to the share purchase method, but there are other differences too, such as:

- Obviously, a share repurchase by the corporation does not bring in any new shareholders; and

- Share repurchase may have unintended results regarding voting control. If, for example, ABCD Ltd has the following shareholders:

- A: 40%

- B: 30%

- C: 20%

- D: 10%

Then shareholder A can be outvoted by the other three. If shareholder B dies and his shares are redeemed by ABCD Ltd., then the revised shareholdings would be:

- A: 57%

- C: 29%

- D: 14%

Shareholder A now has voting control of the corporation. If this was intended, all well and good. If not, then share repurchase should not have been used.

- Share repurchase may run afoul of the restrictions imposed by any creditor of the corporation. Loan documents typically prohibit share repurchase by the corporation without specific written permission from the lender;

- Cross-purchase has an element of simplicity that is still attractive to many clients. At times, the intricacies of corporate share repurchase can be intimidating and clients may be reluctant to just hand over everything to their accounting and legal advisors; and

- For businesses whose shareholders might each fit within the SBGE limits, share repurchase may, initially at least, be unnecessarily complex and costly. For a newly incorporated company, for example, it will in all likelihood be some time before the SBGE limits are exceeded, so cross-purchase will be more efficient from a tax point of view.

From a tax point of view, it is essential for an advisor to appreciate the fundamental differences between share purchase and corporate share repurchase. A simplified example will serve to illustrate the major points:

Business: XY Ltd

Shareholders:

- X — 50%

- Y — 50%

Business value: $1,000,000.

Adjusted cost base: $0*

Shareholder Y dies.

Paid up capital value: $0*

Step 1 applies to both share repurchase and cross purchase.

Paragraph 70(5)(a) of the *Income Tax Act* provides that, in the event of the death of a taxpayer, "the taxpayer shall be deemed to have, immediately before the taxpayer's death, disposed of each capital property of the tax-payer and received proceeds of disposition therefor equal to the fair market value of the property immediately before the death".

So, on Y's death, he is deemed to have disposed of his shares in XY Ltd for $500,000 (fair market value immediately before his death), and will be taxed accordingly.

Y is deemed to have disposed of his shares to his estate, in effect, at fair market value ($500,000). This is specified by paragraph 70(5)(b): "any person who as a consequence of the taxpayer's death acquires any property that is deemed by paragraph (a) to have been disposed of by the taxpayer shall be deemed to have acquired it at the time of the death at a cost equal to its fair market value immediately before the death".

It is important to recognize that Y and his estate are two separate and distinct taxpayers and that each will be taxed as such.

To summarize Step 1:

- Y dies;

- Y is deemed to have disposed of his shares in XY Ltd for $500,000;

- Y's estate is deemed to have acquired Y's shares in XY Ltd for $500,000; and

- Tax implications:

---

* Will usually be nominal, but greater than $0.

Y's proceeds of disposition:	$500,000
ACB:	0
Capital Gain:	500,000
Estate's interest in XY Ltd.:	500,000
Estate's ACB:	500,000

Step 2 will vary according to the buyer.

If shareholder X is the buyer:

Purchase price to X:	$500,000
ACB to X:	500,000
Estate's proceeds of disposition:	500,000
Estates's ACB:	500,000
Estate's capital gain:	0

If XY Ltd is the buyer:

When a corporation buys back its own shares, it is deemed to pay a dividend to the extent that the purchase price exceeds the paid-up capital value of the shares (subsection 84(3) of the Act).

If the amount so paid is considered by the Act to be a dividend, then it follows that the same amount cannot also be a capital payment (generally, an amount may be income or capital, but cannot be both).

Section 54 of the Act defines "Proceeds of disposition" and excludes "any amount that would otherwise be proceeds of disposition of a share to the extent that the amount is deemed by subsection 84(2) or (3) to be a dividend received and is not deemed by paragraph 55(2)(*a*) or subparagraph 88(2)(*b*)(ii) not to be a dividend" (subparagraph (*j*)). So, the estate is deemed to have sold the shares to XY Ltd. for a dividend which is not to be treated as capital.

To summarize this step for the repurchase options:

Sale price by estate:	$500,000	
Paid up capital value:	0	
Deemed dividend:	500,000	(subsection 84(3))
Proceeds of disposition:	0	(proceeds minus dividend) (section 54)
ACB of shares to estate:	500,000	(from step 1)
Capital loss to estate:	500,000	

Step 3 applies only to corporate share repurchase:

We now have Y reporting a capital gain of $500,000 on his terminal return.

We also have Y's estate reporting a capital loss of $500,000 triggered by the deemed dividend rule.

We have a $500,000 gain and a $500,000 loss, but two separate and distinct taxpayers. Here, subsection 164(6) comes to the rescue, and provides that, as long as everything is completed within the first taxation year of the estate, then the loss realized by the estate may be considered to be a loss realized by the taxpayer.

Without this special provision, the $500,000 payment would be taxed as a capital gain on Y's terminal return and as a dividend on his estate's tax return, so the effective tax rate would be about 45%. Therefore, the application of 164(6) is a crucial step, and it should be noted that the "carry back" is available only within the first taxation year of the estate — any undue delay could be disastrous.

In fact, the $500,000 could ultimately be taxed three times: in the hands of the deceased shareholder, in his estate, and again in the hands of the surviving shareholder, who receives no step-up in ACB.

If for any reason the one-year time limit is approaching and obstacles still block the redemption route, then it would be prudent for the surviving shareholder to step in and buy the deceased's shares from the estate. There would be no capital gain in the estate, which has an ACB of $500,000 for the shares. The surviving shareholder would then have an ACB of $500,000 for the shares, so the amount would only be taxed once.

To summarize the difference between cross purchase and corporate share repurchase for X, Y, and XY Ltd.:

On Y's death:

	Cross purchase by X	Share repurchase by XY Ltd
Deemed disposition by Y	$500,000	$500,000
ACB of shares	0	0
Capital gain of Y	500,000	500,000

	Cross purchase by X	Share repurchase by XY Ltd
Estate ACB of shares	500,000	500,000
Sale to X	500,000	
Gain to estate	0	
Sale to XY Ltd		500,000
Deemed dividend		500,000
Estate proceeds of disposition		0
Estate capital loss		(500,000)
Carry-back to Y's gain		(500,000)
Net capital gain to Y	500,000	0
Tax at 20%	100,000	0
Net cash from sale	400,000	
Taxable dividend in estate	0	500,000
Tax at 25%	0	125,000
Net cash from repurchase	0	375,000
Increase in ACB to X	500,000	0

In this example, the bottom line of the comparison is a $25,000 tax penalty on share repurchase, and a loss of $500,000 of ACB increase for X, which is a double penalty.

Note that the above comparison makes no reference to financing costs, and specifically no reference to life insurance funding, which changes the comparison significantly.

Similarly, the availability of the Small Business Gains Exemption would have a major impact in this type of situation. Utilizing corporate share repurchase would be a very expensive option, as it would replace a tax-free capital gain with a taxable dividend.

Stop-Loss Rules

If we take the case study of XY Ltd. to the next step, it would be prudent to look at where the cash to make the purchase will come from. The logical solution when considering a purchase of shares on death is to use life insurance, so that the event that creates the problem will also create the cash to solve the problem.

The Capital Dividend Account

Subsection 89(1) of the *Income Tax Act* provides that the Capital Dividend Account (CDA) of a private corporation at any particular time consists of:

- The non-taxable portion (currently 50%) of net capital gains;

- Capital dividends received from other private corporations; and

- Life insurance proceeds received by the corporation, to the extent that they exceed the ACB of the policy to the corporation.

The CDA is not an actual account of the corporation, but is a notional account with special properties. Subsection 83(2) provides that, where a corporation makes the appropriate election specifying that a particular dividend is to be treated as a capital dividend, "no part of the dividend shall be included in computing the income of any shareholder of the corporation" (s. 83(2)(*b*)).

Although the CDA is created by, for instance, life insurance proceeds, its existence does not depend on maintaining these proceeds in cash in the corporation. As an example, if XY Ltd. were to buy a $1,000,000 life insurance policy to cover a specific bank loan, then on Y's death it would receive $1,000,000 cash, tax free. It would then use the cash to repay the bank loan. But the CDA would still show a credit of $1,000,000 less the ACB of the policy to the corporation, even though there is no cash left. The CDA remains until it is used up by the corporation making a specific election to pay a capital dividend.

The CDA in Corporate Share Repurchase (Pre-Stop-Loss)

Returning to the example of XY Ltd., when the corporation buys back its shares from Y's estate, it is deemed to pay a dividend of $500,000 minus the paid-up capital value of the shares (assumed for this example to be $0, although in reality there would be some nominal paid-up capital amount). So if XY Ltd. had a credit of $500,000 in its CDA, could it elect that the dividend deemed to be paid should come from the CDA and therefore be non-taxable? If so, then the repurchase transaction would look as follows:

Capital gain to Y: $500,000 (deemed disposition)

Deemed dividend to estate

                                       Proceeds $500,000

                                       PUCV $0

                                       $500,000

Proceeds of disposition to estate

                                       Proceeds $500,000

                                       Minus dividend $500,000

                                       $0

Capital loss to estate

                                       Proceeds $0

                                       ACB $500,000

                                       $500,000

Net gain to Y

                                       Gain to Y $500,000*

                                       Loss in estate $500,000*

Dividend to Estate

                                       Deemed Dividend $500,000

                                       Via CDA $500,000

                                       Taxable Dividend $0**

The end result is that no tax is payable by Y or by his estate, a result made possible by the CDA created by life insurance proceeds payable to XY Ltd.

Reducing the Loss Available

In 1995, rules were put forward whose intention was to remove some of the advantage outlined in the previous section above. It was felt that having the entire corporate repurchase transaction take place without any tax whatsoever was not an equitable position. The proposed rules changed several times before they were finally enacted in 1998, and in this final form they provide that, in a corporate share repurchase situation, any capital loss

---

* Subsection 164(6) of the *Income Tax Act.*

** Section 83(2)(*b*) of the *Income Tax Act.*

realized by the estate (and any loss deemed to be the individual's loss) will be reduced.

The amount of the reduction in this capital loss will be calculated as:

(1) The lesser of

    (a) capital dividend received by the estate on the shares;

    (b) the loss otherwise determined, minus taxable dividends received;

(2) minus 50% of the lesser of

    (a) the loss otherwise determined;

    (b) the individual's capital gain realized on death;

In the above example, the estate received a $500,000 dividend from the CDA and was then able to "carry back" a loss of $500,000 to cancel out Y's $500,000 capital gain. Under the new rules, the $500,000 "carry back" would be reduced by:

(1) the lesser of

    (a) capital dividends received by the estate: $500,000;

    (b) the loss otherwise determined: $500,000;

(2) minus 50% of the lesser of

    (a) the loss otherwise determined: $500,000;

    (b) the individual's gain realized on death : $500,000;

This translates into a reduction of:

    (i) $500,000

    (ii) minus 50% of $500,000

The loss available for "carry back" is reduced to $250,000 (i.e., the loss is reduced by $250,000).

This will leave $250,000 of gain on Y's terminal tax return, with tax of around $50,000 at a marginal rate of 40%.

In essence, this "wastes" $250,000 of CDA, since the tax-free dividend simply increases the amount of taxable gain.

The "50% Solution"

This approach involves having XY Ltd. elect that only 50% of the deemed dividend will be from the CDA. If XY Ltd. paid only $250,000 as a capital dividend, then the loss carried back would not be reduced (the stop-loss calculation has a built-in allowance for 50% of the individual gain). This means that Y's estate would be paid a combination of taxable and non-taxable dividends, and that Y's terminal return would have no capital gain to be taxed.

Of course, if XY Ltd. only pays $250,000 of CDA and $250,000 of taxable dividend, then the corporation still has a CDA credit of $250,000 for the benefit of surviving shareholders. In a way, this is the trade-off for X having no increase in ACB in a corporate share repurchase.

"Grandfathering"

The stop-loss rules apply to any corporate share repurchase situation, so they would produce inequities for situations already in place. Accordingly, there are exceptions:

(i) If the share repurchase is made pursuant to a written agreement entered into prior to April 27, 1995, then the stop-loss rules will not apply; and

(ii) If the corporation purchasing the shares was a beneficiary of a life insurance policy on April 26, 1995, and one of the main purposes of the policy was to fund the repurchase of shares held on April 26, 1995 by the life insured, the life insured's spouse or the life insured's estate, then the stop-loss rules will not apply.

So, the "old" system of corporate share repurchase with no current tax liability is still available if an arrangement is "grandfathered". A great deal has been written about the rules, and a number of grey areas still exist, probably to be resolved by the courts in the future, but some general conclusions can be drawn in this context:

- If grandfathering is claimed on the basis of an in-force agreement prior to April 27, 1995, then the agreement must still be in force at the time of the repurchase. Any substantial changes to the agreement could jeopardize the grandfathering (although there is as yet no real consensus on what types of changes would constitute "substantial changes");

- If grandfathering is claimed on the basis of life insurance being in place for share repurchase funding on April 26, 1995, then there is no requirement that the policy still be in place at any point in the future. The policy itself may be replaced, cancelled, modified, increased or decreased without any adverse effect on the grandfathered status; and

- If grandfathered status is available because of the life insurance policy, then changes can be made to the agreement without fear of negative impact on that side. Great care should be taken in determining that grandfathered status does indeed exist in any particular situation, and comprehensive documentation of the status should be maintained. It is possible that share repurchases made 30, 40 or more years from now will be governed by these rules, long after the principals involved have forgotten all of the discussions that took place. During the planning process, these issues must be resolved with some certainty, documented and incorporated into the plans being made at the time. In many cases, it would be difficult, if not impossible, to go back decades and try to re-construct the process.

Life Insurance Funding

There is no doubt that life insurance funding is the most efficient way to provide cash to the purchaser of shares when the purchase is triggered by the death of a shareholder. That is, of course, as long as the funding is arranged correctly. When clients and their advisors sit down to discuss this aspect of succession planning, questions that must be considered in order to arrive at an optimum solution will include:

(a) Is life insurance the best solution in this particular situation?

(b) If so, what kind of life insurance should be used?

(c) How much insurance is necessary?

(d) What if a shareholder is uninsurable?

(e) Who should own the life insurance?

With the many developments that have taken place in the life insurance industry in recent years, the topic is much more complex than can be addressed in this brief chapter, but we will focus on the five topics listed above.

Is Life Insurance the Best Solution in this Situation?

Returning to the XY Ltd. example, someone needs $500,000 to buy Y's shares on death, either X or XY Ltd.

At age 50 today, Y probably has an average life expectancy of about 30 years. If we knew exactly how long he would live, then it would be easy to make all the right decisions, but for now we have to make some assumptions and then test the implications of those assumptions.

At one extreme, Y could be run over by a truck and killed tomorrow. In that case, life insurance purchased today would be a spectacular investment. Even the most uncompetitive insurance product would produce a rate of return of many, many thousands of percentage points.

At the other extreme, if Y lived to age 80, we have to look at what the alternatives would have been.

Over the 30-year period, prudent planning would mean that XY Ltd. (or X, whoever is the purchaser) could decide on the following alternatives:

(i)   Accumulating the $500,000 required in a "sinking fund";

(ii) Do nothing, then borrow $500,000 in the event of Y's death; and

(iii) Buy life insurance today.

The "Sinking Fund" is Usually a Notional Measurement Only, Since it Would Be an Unlikely Course of Action in the Real World

If XY Ltd. could invest cash annually in a sinking fund to earn, say, 6% which would be taxed at 48% (since it is not active business income), it would have to invest the following amounts, on the assumption that the cash would not be needed until 30 years from now:

Number of deposits	Present value at 6% pre-tax, 2.922% after tax
30 × 10,341	210,728
20 × 13,663	210,728
10 × 23,907	210,728

While not necessarily a practical course of action, this calculation gives us a benchmark against which to measure other alternatives. If, for example, a particular alternative had a higher cost than this, then we could safely ignore that alternative.

Borrow When Necessary

If XY Ltd. were to borrow $500,000 30 years from now, and then repay the loan over 10 years at 6% interest (probably deductible interest), then loan repayments would average $58,975 annually, after tax. The advantage of this method is that it requires no action now. Its cost would be measured as the cost of loan repayment, discounted to today's value at the same net interest used in the "Sinking Fund" section above (6% pre-tax, 3.12% after tax).

Year	Outlay
1–30	$ 0
31–40	$61,339

Present Value: $270,466.

Temporary Insurance (Term Insurance)

If we are safe in the assumption that Y should live to about age 80, then we can consider term life coverage for the funding.

Representative annual premium costs for $500,000 on Y's life, based on a healthy non-smoker, would be:

- Age 50-59 — $1,200 annually;
- Age 60-69 — $6,000 annually;
- Age 70-79 — $16,000 annually;

Looking at the same present value approach as in the other two alternatives:

- $1,200 annually × 10 years = 10,491;
- 6,000 annually × 10 years = 52,456 discounted a further 10 yrs = 38,580;
- 16,000 annually × 10 years = 139,884 discounted a further 20 yrs = 75,667;
- Total present value = $124,738;

This present value cost of $124,738 compares with $198,921 for the "sinking fund" approach and $270,466 for the borrowing approach. This is a very significant difference, but of course this is not yet a fair comparison, since:

- The "sinking fund" is intact at any time after age 80;

- Bank borrowing is not time-sensitive, other than for the usual interest rate fluctuations;

- Term insurance will expire at age 80, even if Y does not. XY Ltd. would run the risk of having no funding in place. This temporary approach to funding is often merely a "band aid" solution until some other alternative is forced into place by a change of circumstances. This often leads to a revised approach of "buy term and invest the difference," combining, for example, the sinking fund and the life insurance.

Permanent Insurance

The life insurance industry has always displayed a good deal of creativity in naming its policies and policy types. Unfortunately, the creativity has done little to help a general understanding of the alternatives. For the purposes of this discussion, we will use the term "permanent insurance" to mean simply life insurance that will not expire.

XY Ltd. could purchase $500,000 of life insurance on Y for about $5,500 annually, payable for Y's lifetime. Up to age 80, this outlay would have a net present value of $106,149. If Y lived to age 90, the present value of total premium deposits would be $124,701, so this type of funding is effective and efficient regardless of duration.

If XY Ltd. wanted to limit its premium paying period, then the life insurance could be designed to be fully paid after, say, 20 years or even a much shorter period such as five or 10 years. Present value costs would not change significantly, although actual dollar amounts would vary considerably.

The point of the comparison is that life insurance is a more certain and more economical way of funding a buyout on death than any of the usual alternatives. In addition, life insurance has the extra advantage of creating Capital Dividend Account, with its accompanying tax advantages.

To answer the question "Is life insurance the best solution in this situation?" the answer is a clear and unmistakable "yes".

What Kind of Life Insurance Should Be Used?

While this current analysis is not intended to examine in detail all available types of life insurance, there are, even from the above comparisons, certain conclusions to be drawn:

- Temporary insurance (term insurance) can be an effective interim solution, but loses all its advantages if the insured outlives the coverage. Typically, term insurance expires at age 75 to 80 (often prior to average life expectancy);

- Permanent insurance (which would include such generic types as whole life insurance, universal life insurance, Term to 100 insurance and so on) provides an effective long-term solution, regardless of how long the insured lives. The initial cost is higher than that of term insurance, but on a long-term basis it has a clear advantage;

- If life insurance is purchased to fund a share purchase, whether by X or by XY Ltd., the presence or absence of cash values is not particularly relevant unless they are an integral part of any financing package being negotiated. At its simplest, life insurance is purchased to provide tax-free cash on death. Once the decision to purchase life insurance is made, then the potential advantages of a policy with cash values can be reviewed. The comparison, however, is not between "term" insurance and "cash value" insurance, but between "temporary" and "permanent" life insurance. Once that is resolved, then the cash value issue may be addressed;

- The advantages of a "quick pay" life insurance policy can be significant. If, for example, Y plans on retiring at age 60, or at least semi-retiring, then he might feel more comfortable knowing that the insurance on his life is fully paid at age 60. Typically, a "quick pay" life insurance policy tends to have more flexibility, such as being able to skip a premium deposit if cash flow is tight, or double up if cash is plentiful. Similarly, the policy owner might be able to elect to stop payments altogether and take a smaller policy. As an example, if Y were to be bought out by X over a period of time, then X might decide to reduce the insurance coverage as the buyout takes place;

    As a unique financial instrument, life insurance is now very "customer driven" and very flexible. It can be custom tailored to fit any imaginable situation.

- As an interesting aside, even if XY Ltd. were to have on hand sufficient cash to write Y's estate a cheque for $500,000, it might still be appropriate for them to buy life insurance to fund the share purchase. The innate cost efficiency of life insurance itself, combined with the favourable tax treatment that results, mean that life insurance is quite simply a better financial solution to the problem.

How Much Insurance is Necessary?

If life insurance is a more efficient funding medium than the other available alternatives, then it is logical that all of the purchase price should be life insured. The concept of buying life insurance for the first $200,000 or $300,000, then self-funding the balance, for example, simply does not make economic sense (unless the objective is to pay as little as possible by way of life insurance premiums, rather than to solve the funding problem in the most efficient way).

Since the Capital Dividend Account credit is calculated as life insurance proceeds in excess of the adjusted cost base (ACB) of the policy, then consideration should be given to designing a policy where the death benefit at any given time is the stated face amount (in this case, $500,000) plus the ACB of the policy. If, for example, Y were to die in the tenth year of the policy, when the policy ACB was $5,000, the death benefit would be $505,000, so that the CDA credit would be the desired $500,000.

Another crucial issue revolves around the market value of the shares. If they have a value of $500,000 today, how much life insurance coverage should be purchased? If Y dies tomorrow, the $500,000 should still be sufficient, but then of course if he is about to die tomorrow, it is unlikely that he could get the insurance coverage today. Over time, share value will fluctuate. X and Y hope that it will tend to increase rather than remain constant or decrease. Faced with this probability, X and Y have another choice to make, based on the following alternatives:

(i) Over-insure today. If Y is insurable, XY Ltd. could buy $750,000 or $1,000,000 of coverage, which would provide room for growth. This alternative would involve the co-operation of the insurer in issuing more than is actually required, and would carry the additional cost of paying for $250,000 or $500,000 of coverage that is not needed yet;

(ii) Index the insurance amount. Some insurers provide the option of increasing the coverage by, say 5% or 10% annually. While not an exact tracking of share value, this can often be preferable to remaining at a fixed insurance amount; and

(iii) Tie the insurance amount to share value. While not as widely available as simple indexing, it is possible to use life insurance coverage that will adjust periodically to match share value. Typically, such coverage does have some limitations, such as a maximum increase of about 25% per year, but it offers a tremendous advantage over more traditional funding vehicles. Maximum coverage amounts available could be as high as $50,000,000.

The key consideration in this area is insurability. If Y can qualify for life insurance today, will he also qualify next year, or five or 10 years from now? Many business life insurance agreements are put together on the assumption that each shareholder will simply increase the insurance amount whenever share value changes, but this rarely, if ever, works in practice. For various reasons, share valuations are not done regularly, people put off going for insurance medicals until they lose a few pounds or until they are more relaxed after they vacation or until they quit smoking. Eventually, people become uninsurable, and whatever can be done in advance to maximize the adequacy and flexibility of insurance coverage should be seriously considered.

What If a Shareholder is Uninsurable?

Sometimes, even early in the planning stages, it is discovered that a shareholder cannot qualify for life insurance. This may be for reasons of health (illness, high blood pressure, obesity), avocation (sky-diving instructor, shark trainer) or lifestyle (weekly speeding tickets, drug use) and requires creative problem-solving on everyone's part.

It is sometimes possible to use other coverage already in place on the uninsurable shareholder's life, but of course this takes away coverage from some other area and is not always feasible.

If appropriate, it may be possible to re-orient the business funding need. As an example, if Y were found to be uninsurable, then it might be possible to insure his wife instead. On Y's death, he would leave his shares to his wife on a tax-free rollover. Perhaps the shares would be re-organized so that she would receive preferred shares at a fixed value, possibly with dividend rights attached. Ultimately, on Mrs. Y's death, the shares would go to whomever they were originally intended for, and life insurance proceeds could be the funding medium.

This type of arrangement requires a special type of situation and cannot routinely be used in the majority of arm's length succession plans. It can, however, be a useful tool when other alternatives are unavailable.

Who Should Own the Life Insurance?

In XY Ltd., if the plan agreed upon is a share repurchase plan, then the insurance proceeds need to find their way to XY Ltd. This does not necessarily mean that XY Ltd. is the owner. The policy on Y's life could be owned by XY Ltd, by X, or even by Y, or by a holding company.

Consider the following structure:

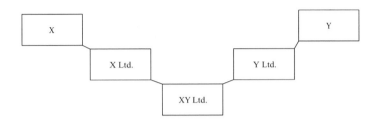

If insurance on Y's life were owned by Y Ltd., then the following advantages would result:

- Money for premium payments could be paid to Y Ltd. from XY Ltd. as tax-free inter-corporate dividends;

- If XY Ltd. is named beneficiary, then it would receive proceeds tax-free on Y's death. Since XY Ltd. has no ACB in the policy, it is possible that all proceeds would go into the Capital Dividend Account of XY Ltd. without ACB erosion. Care should be taken to ensure that this is not the primary motivation for the structure, and that other valid business reasons exist for Y Ltd.;

- If X and Y decide to part company, or if some third party wants to buy Y's interest in the business, then the insurance policy would remain intact in Y Ltd. rather than in XY Ltd.; and

- Y Ltd. may offer some security from XY Ltd.'s creditors, subject to personal and corporate guarantees.

Generally, corporate ownership of life insurance funding would allow premium payments to be made with cheaper dollars, since premiums are non-deductible and would be paid after tax at, say, 20% rather than 40%.

Personal ownership may afford some element of creditor protection, however, and should not be overlooked, especially in high-risk or litigation prone industries.

CHAPTER 5

Family Owned Businesses

Special Considerations

The statistics regarding the survival of family businesses from one generation to the next are not very encouraging. On a consistent basis, the survival rate averages around 30%. Starting from 10 family business enterprises today, we would expect three to survive to the second generation, and one to survive to the third generation. When dealing with family businesses, advisors need to pay special attention to some of the key differences compared with non-family businesses.

Family Dynamics

Many family-owned businesses operate 24 hours a day. They do not necessarily intend to, but family get-togethers, dinners, golf games and trips to hockey games can all too easily turn into business discussions. Decisions made one afternoon are often changed the following morning, after family members have had further discussion. The business becomes all-encompassing, and the distinction between business and family all but disappears.

In this context, all of the normal "rivalries" or differences that arise in any business environment are magnified many times. Imagine having a bad day at work and then having no escape when you go home.

If advisors fail to take this into account in the planning process, problems are unavoidable. The mechanics of a succession plan have to take second place to the "feel" of the plan to the family members, even to those not directly involved.

Tradition

In a family business environment, there is often a strong desire to do things the way they have always been done. The predominance of names like "Brown and Sons" or "Jones and Son", is a clear indication of the traditional influence. The business world has changed dramatically in recent years, and it is continuing to change at a pace that seems to be accelerating (however impossible that seems at times). This change is difficult to cope with, but is especially difficult in a family business scenario.

A recent study conducted by the Deloitte and Touche Centre for Tax Education and Research at the University of Waterloo highlights the scope of the problem:

- More than half of the family businesses surveyed will have their leader retire within 10 years. Within 15 years, more than 75% will retire;

- Most admit that no contingency plan is in place, and have made no decision about how to even go about the task of selecting a successor. This complacency is dangerous, and one of the most important functions of an advisor to a family business is to provide some motivation, some incentive to get the process started. (See Chapter 14, "How to Get Started", as well as the CIBC World Markets survey from 2005, outlined in Chapter 16, "The Business Owner's

Perspective", whose findings mirror those of the University of Waterloo study.)

Expectations

It is not uncommon for family-owned businesses to be hampered by unreasonable expectations. If John Smith, the founder of the business, was a wonderful, dynamic business leader with a real "vision", it does not follow that his son or daughter will have the same strengths. Yet it is not uncommon to see the oldest child being pulled to follow in father's footsteps, while younger siblings are denied the same consideration.

An only child has a particularly difficult time ignoring the pressure. Will this continue to be a family business or not? Another source of unreasonable expectations causing conflict can be in the area of finances, specifically regarding salary, bonuses, and dividends. "If Dad's business could afford to pay him a $50,000 bonus and Mom a $20,000 dividend, why can't we do it now?"

"In-laws"

If the Smith family owns Smithco and John Smith marries Suzie Brown, does Suzie become a member of the family business group, or remain an outsider? This type of acceptance/non-acceptance issue is not restricted to a business environment, of course, but it is especially difficult where businesses are involved. If, for example, John Smith Senior completes an estate freeze and gives growth shares to John Smith Junior, then is Junior allowed to will the shares to Suzie in the event of his death? If so, then what happens if Suzie remarries? Could Smithco end up being owned by complete strangers?

This kind of topic can make for some interesting, although not necessarily enjoyable, dinner-table conversations. It can also provide advisors with some significant obstacles to navigate around. Again, the advisor must be aware of the existence of this type of obstacle and must be prepared to raise the issue if necessary.

Treating Family Members Fairly

In a typical family business succession plan, one of the most delicate balancing acts is deciding how to treat family members both inside and outside the business.

As a simple example, assume that Father runs the family business, Son works in the business and Daughter is a nurse. When Father decides to do an estate freeze, he can issue common shares to Son. Should he also give shares to Daughter? She does not work in the business, so he decides not to give her any shares.

In his will, he leaves his shares in Opco to Son. How should he treat Daughter in this case?

There is often a big difference between "fair" and "equal", although the difference is not always agreed upon. It is not uncommon for one parent to insist that the children should be treated fairly, while the other insists that they should be treated equally.

Leaving the business equally to Son and Daughter can be a recipe for disaster, even if Son has voting control. Son, for example, may want to re-invest profits to grow the company, while Daughter would want to receive dividend income.

Equalizing by some other method may be possible, such as leaving Son the business and leaving Daughter other assets, but, of course, as business value becomes more significant, this alternative becomes less practical.

While not an easy process, it is essential for the family to discuss this "fair or equal" concept during the planning stages. The role of the advisor might then be to facilitate such a discussion, perhaps acting as a moderator, since many business owners feel uncomfortable even bringing up such a topic for discussion. The agenda for this type of meeting might be expressed as: "Father is in the process of doing some estate planning. As you would expect, a major factor is what he should do with the business. Since Son is working in the business, he would be a logical successor, but we don't want to be unfair to Daughter. What do you think would be a fair way for us to handle this?"

The result of this discussion can be surprising, as children usually sympathize with the parents' dilemma and are eager to find a good solution. Petty jealousies and competitiveness tend to disappear, much to the parents' relief. The alternative, having the parents make a decision on their own, can be intimidating and destructive to the business and the family.

Sometimes, a "tidy" solution is simply nowhere to be found, for all kinds of reasons, and then the only recourse is to find the solution that does the least amount of damage. The importance of open discussion within the family cannot be over-emphasized.

Capital or Income Transactions?

If the founder and sole owner of what he hopes will become a family business decides to retire, is it necessary for him to sell his shares to the next generation? Does he need capital, or would an income stream be an acceptable alternative? There is, of course, no "right" answer to this type of question, but it is a question that should be asked.

If Senior owns a business worth $2,000,000, is it reasonable to expect his children to pay $2,000,000 to acquire it? Where would they get the money?

It would be reasonable to assume a tax liability of around $300,000, so, even if he sold it for cash, Senior would net only $1,700,000, which he would then invest at, say, 6%. This would provide him with an income of around $102,000 pre-tax. Instead, his children could agree to pay him, say, $100,000 per year for life, or indeed an amount that would vary with investment yields over the years.

In his will, Senior will leave the business to:

(a) His wife, or

(b) His children.

If it goes to his wife, he would leave her his shares (no tax) and she would continue to receive the agreed upon annual income.

On her death, or if he leaves the shares directly to his children, the $300,000 tax bill will become payable. His children could then be responsible for the tax bill. They will pay $1,700,000 less than they would have if they had purchased the shares, Senior will have received exactly the same income, and the tax bill would remain the same. Of course, the timing of the tax would be different, as it would not have been paid in advance. This example assumes capital gains exemption availability.

Funding the Tax

Following up on the earlier discussion of share repurchase strategies, the tax payable in this example could be reduced as well as funded by the use of life insurance.

As an example, the $300,000 tax liability could be handled as follows, assuming the $2,000,000 value is in fixed value preferred shares.

(a) Seniorco buys $300,000 of life insurance on the life of Senior. On his death, the $300,000 is paid to Seniorco and creates CDA credit (less the ACB of the policy to Seniorco). The shares pass to the children, who then declare a dividend to themselves via the CDA, enabling them to pay the tax;

(b) Seniorco insures Senior for $300,000. On his death, Seniorco redeems $300,000 of shares from his estate. The remaining shares are left to the children, along with the net proceeds of the share repurchase; and

(c) Seniorco insures Senior for $300,000. On his death, Seniorco redeems $1,500,000 of shares from his estate (for $300,000 cash and a $1,200,000 promissory note) and wills the remaining $500,000 to the children.

From the children's point of view, the end result of these methods is quite different:

	ACB of shares to children	Promissory note to children	Tax paid
A	$2,000,000	0	500,000
B	$1,500,000	0	375,000
C	$ 500,000	1,200,000	465,000

Interestingly, alternative C gives the children the opportunity to receive up to $1,200,000 tax free from Seniorco in the future as repayment of the promissory note. This has a more practical value than a higher ACB, which is of course a benefit only when shares are sold. Note that, in some instances, it could be argued that a promissory note may constitute control of a corporation and may lead to stop-loss problems. Care should be taken in this area. Generally, a demand promissory note entails more risk than a note with specified terms of repayment.

The choice as to which of the above methods makes sense depends on many factors, of course, and there is danger is oversimplification, but it may be counter-productive to assume that there is only one way to use life insurance proceeds to pay tax.

Family Trusts

In essence, a trust is a vehicle to allow for the transfer of property without deciding all the details of ownership. In a family business, a trust is often used to provide extra time for making the "fair vs. equal" kind of decision.

In the above example, Senior could leave his shares in Seniorco to a trust whose beneficiaries are his children. If the trust is discretionary, then there is no need for him to decide at once who should receive what portion of the business. While this is typically a mechanism to be used as part of an estate freeze (see Chapter 8, "Estate Freezing") it can also provide a temporary solution here.

If, for example, Senior were to establish a trust in favour of his children, and transfer some shares to the trust (no rollover is available, so they would be newly issued shares or shares to trigger the SBGE amount), then the trust could own the shares instead of the children owning them. At any time in the next 21 years, the shares could be distributed to the beneficiaries in any proportion, even to the extreme of excluding one or more beneficiaries. The beneficiaries would then receive the shares on a rollover basis, at the same ACB as when the shares were put into the trust. Meanwhile, the trust allows Senior to decide who should own the shares.

In past years, family trusts have been used extensively for the purpose of income splitting, "sprinkling" dividends among family members to reduce the overall tax burden on earnings from a business of professional practice. As attribution rules have become more far-reaching, income splitting has become more difficult, particularly where minor children are involved. As an estate planning or business succession planning tool, however, trusts have lost none of their popularity.

Family Law Considerations

While it is not the purpose of this book to provide an analysis of family law legislation in Canada, any advisor should at least be aware of some of the pitfalls.

The discussion of "fair vs. equal" is made more complicated by the existence of family law, and indeed by the changing view of the courts in general of what constitutes fair treatment of shareholders, spouses, children, and siblings.

It would be imprudent to ignore "fairness" when planning for business succession within a family enterprise. Since "fairness" is such a subjective concept, this would be a strong argument in favour of shareholder agreements, even within a family group. As usual, it is the discussion and negotiation leading up to the preparation of the agreement that helps to crystallize the thoughts of the participants.

Marriage break-up can always be a threat to ongoing business viability, and it is not uncommon to see a divorce or any action under the *Family Law Act* of a province be listed as a "triggering" event in a shareholder agreement. This type of solution carries with it a great number of problems too, but is evidently preferable to seeing a percentage of the shares in the family business pass outside the family, where they could even pass to total strangers in the event of a remarriage.

When parents pass shares to children, whether as an estate planning exercise or as a business, they will invariably be concerned when the children get married. In the event of a marriage break-up, then how would the shares be handled?

If provincial law does not offer any protection for the shares, as is the case in Ontario, for example, then consideration should be given to drawing up a marriage contract.

This type of concern could also be resolved (for a while, at least) by having shares in a discretionary trust rather than held by children directly. Marriage or divorce would generally have no impact on share ownership or entitlement as long as the shares are in a trust with no guarantee of their ultimate distribution to a particular individual. Once shares are distributed, of course, then protection disappears, but the trust can provide up to 21 years of peace of mind in this context.

CHAPTER 6

Small Business
Gains Exemption

T he *Income Tax Act* provides that an individual resident in Canada may realize up to $500,000 of capital gain from the sale of shares of a Qualified Small Business Corporation (QSBC) without any tax liability. Since this is not a deferment of tax, but an outright exemption, it follows that a typical shareholder will be vitally interested in taking advantage of it as soon as possible.

Qualification

This Small Business Gains Exemption (SBGE) is available as long as the corporation whose shares are in question meets the definition of a QSBC:

- It is a Canadian-controlled private corporation (CCPC); and

- All or substantially all of its assets are used in an active business carried on primarily in Canada. This is normally considered as at least 90% of the fair market value of its assets.

Note that the exemption will not be available if the corporation is not an active business. This can be particularly troublesome if the planning is taking place as an active business is winding down and making the unavoidable transition to inactive, investing proceeds from the sale of assets in real estate or term deposits, and becoming an investor rather than a provider of goods and services.

If the corporation itself qualifies as a QSBC, then the next step is to determine whether the shares qualify for the exemption at the time of the proposed disposition:

- The shares were not held by anyone other than the taxpayer or related persons over the last 24 months;

- Throughout that 24-month period, at least 50% of the fair market value of its assets was used in an active business conducted primarily in Canada; and

- Throughout the 24-month period, the company is a CCPC.

In those instances where the SBGE is not available for a given transaction, it is most often because of a failure to pass the "90% test" at the time of the disposition, or the "50% test" over the preceding 24 months. Where this is the case, the problem is often capable of solution.

Purification

The asset tests referred to above are based on the fair market value of assets. No reference is made to liabilities, nor to net assets. Where an examination of the assets of a corporation reveals that the test is failed, then the "purification" process might include any of the following steps, among others:

(i) Surplus cash (over and above a temporary excess or a financial "cushion" of a reasonable amount) would constitute a "non qualifying" asset, especially if used to earn investment income. To solve this cash problem, a corporation could:

- Pay a taxable dividend to shareholders;

- Pay a capital dividend, if available;

- Repay a bank debt (perhaps to be re-borrowed later);

- Pre-pay a business expense;

- Pre-pay tax instalments;

- Purchase business-use assets;

- Lend money to a connected Small Business Corporation;

- Repay shareholder loans.

(ii) Add the value of goodwill to the calculation. While not normally shown as a balance sheet entry, goodwill should qualify as a business use asset. This might involve some valuation expense; and

(iii) Real estate assets can be difficult to categorize as business-use or non-business use assets. If a parcel of land is simply held as an investment, it will appear as a non-business use asset, but if the same parcel were paved as a parking lot for customers of the active business, then it should become a business-use asset.

The area of purification can be complex, and the above issues are intended to be an outline of some of the more common solutions. It should be noted that the 90% test needs to be met only at the time of the disposition of shares, so some element of flexibility is certainly available. As an example, if a corporation could pass an 80% test but not a 90% test, then it might be possible to fix this by having the corporation borrow from a bank to purchase business-use assets. The liability to the bank does not enter into the calculation, just the value of the asset purchased with the borrowed money.

A word of caution on purification, as it is possible to spend more than it is worth. If the tax saving may be 20 or 30 years away, then it may not be worth spending too much of today's dollars on complex valuations and financial adjustments. As in all areas of tax planning, sooner or later, common sense must prevail.

"Locking In"

If you have an opportunity to save $100,000 in taxes at some point in the future, based on rules in effect today, it is natural to want to make sure that saving really is available when it is needed. Tax rules change more frequently than we might wish, and of course we have little direct control over legislative changes, so the concept of "crystallization" or locking in the exemption, may be very attractive.

Suppose X owns 100% of XLtd., with a value of $1,000,000. His son, S, would be a logical successor, and X plans to leave the business to him via his will. At the moment, XLtd. is a QSBC and X's shares will qualify for the SBGE, so in the event of X's death today, the tax calculation would be:

FMV of XLtd.:	$1,000,000
ACB of shares:	0
SBGE:	500,000
Net:	500,000
Taxable gain:	250,000

Without the exemption, of course, the tax bill would double, but X is not ready to dispose of his shares today and has no way of knowing if the exemption will be available in the future.

His motivation to crystallize the exemption is clear, and is worth $100,000 of tax which would effectively be paid by his son in the future.

X decides to do an internal share re-organization under section 86 of the Act. He returns his existing shares to XLtd. for cancellation and has XLtd. issue him new shares with the same $1,000,000 fair market value. Section 86 allows him to do this without incurring tax as long as the ACB of the newly issued shares is $0, the same as the ACB of the old shares, and as long as all of the old shares are exchanged.

In this example, however, X does not want "rollover" treatment, and so elects an ACB of $500,000. This will trigger $500,000 of capital gain, which X will offset by use of the SBGE.

At the end of the process, X will have shares as follows:

Value of XLtd.:	$1,000,000
ACB of shares:	500,000
SBGE available:	0

The SBGE has been converted into an increased ACB, and the end result is that, even if the SBGE were eliminated by future legislation, the ACB of the shares will reflect the value of the SBGE "locking in" the exemption.

Reasons for crystallization would include:

- If XLtd. shares qualify today, they may not in the future if XLtd. acquires more investment assets or ceases to be an active business;

- Legislative changes might eliminate the SBGE; and

- A current non-business asset, insignificant in value today, might grow to the point where it could cause XLtd. to fail the 90% test. This would apply to a corporate-owned life insurance policy, for example.

- There is currently a move to change the capital gains rules and to reduce tax rates — as the tax climate changes, the value of the SBGE will also change, and care should be exercised to ensure that qualifying for the SBGE does not become more trouble than it is worth.

Holding Companies

Opportunities

Combined with estate freezing techniques referred to in Chapter 8, holding companies can provide very valuable planning tools for shareholders. For example, in order to crystallize his SBGE, X could have transferred his shares to a holding company in which other shareholders might include his son.

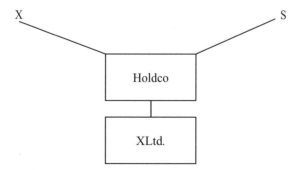

In this type of structure, XLtd. could, for example, flow tax-free dividends to Holdco. Holdco could then purchase investment assets without worrying about what would happen if XLtd. were sold to the mythical multinational corporation with deep pockets. It allows for the separation of business and investment assets.

In addition, if X had other shareholders in XLtd, this type of structure would allow him much more flexibility in terms of introducing other family members as shareholders, as well as providing some opportunity for income splitting where appropriate.

Pitfalls

Having a holding company as the shareholder of XLtd. means that any application of the SBGE could have to take place at the Holdco level, so that if anyone wanted to buy Opco, the SBGE would not be available, since Opco is owned by Holdco and the SBGE is available only to individuals. The same limitation would apply to other shareholders in Holdco, not just to X, so the restriction could be a serious disadvantage.

Multiplying the Exemption

The ability to claim the SBGE two, three, four, or more times within a family unit is a strong argument in favour of planning. If XLtd. were owned by X, his wife, his son, and his daughter, or through a Holdco in which they were shareholders, then they could turn the $500,000 SBGE into a potential $2,000,000 exemption.

Income attribution rules mean that X cannot simply give full value shares to Mrs. X. She would have to actually pay fair market value.

If, however, X decided to establish Holdco as outlined in Chapter 8, then other family members would have the opportunity to use the SBGE when shares increase in value over time.

Points to Consider

The Small Business Gains Exemption can be a source of considerable tax savings of $100,000 per individual taxpayer. Its availability, however, does not mean that it should always be used or relied upon. For example:

- Making the SBGE available to other family members does involve those family members actually owning shares (shares owned by a trust will not be eligible until they are distributed to beneficiaries);

- Using a Holdco may be counter-productive if the SBGE is a central consideration of the planning process;

- If a shareholder agreement calls for shares to be repurchased on death, then the SBGE may, in effect, be wasted (a share repurchase is a dividend transaction, not a capital transaction);

- "Locking in" the exemption today will incur a cost in terms of legal and accounting fees, valuation fees, and so on. These fees should be weighed against the eventual tax saving potential;

- As an extreme view, would it be cheaper, less troublesome or less inconvenient to just purchase an additional $100,000 of life insurance? A biased view, admittedly, but worth considering;

- Alternative Minimum Tax may provide a disincentive to using the SBGE. Even though the AMT would probably be claimed back in future years, the payment of additional tax up front is not an attractive option. For high income earners, earning, say, more than $175,000, AMT is not normally an issue in any event.

CHAPTER 7

Shareholder Agreements

Why Have an Agreement?

A shareholder agreement is to a business what an emergency exit is to a high-rise building. You hope it will not be needed, but it just has to be there.

A wealthy, successful Canadian business owner, who will not be named so as to spare his blushes, once remarked during a meeting of a board of directors on which he served, that a shareholder agreement was the kind of thing that was necessary if the shareholders "did not get along" or "had a

71

problem with each other", and that a shareholder agreement was simply a waste of time and money if the shareholders just respected each other and did what was right. Interesting advice, to be sure, but about as practical as saying you should never buy fire insurance until the house is on fire.

It is precisely because shareholders respect each other that they should enter into a formal, written agreement. When things are going well, discussing some of the more difficult and contentious corporate issues is feasible, though not always enjoyable. When disaster strikes, whether in the form of the death or disability of a shareholder, or in the form of a family "squabble", then the agreement acts as a road map and is often the primary mechanism for dispute resolution.

Typical Provisions and their Importance

There is no "standard" shareholder agreement, and each one should be drafted to address the particular concerns of the individual business in question. There are, however, certain issues that are almost always addressed, such as:

Restriction on Share Transfers

A shareholder cannot arbitrarily sell or give his or her shares to someone else. If a shareholder wants to give shares to his or her children, for example, he or she cannot do so without first obtaining the approval of all other shareholders. This seems fair and appropriate, since shareholders in a closely held corporation need a special "chemistry" for the business to work at its best, and of course this "chemistry" changes when new shareholders appear.

Transfer of Shares to Holding Companies

If a shareholder decides to transfer his or her shares to a holding company (usually for estate planning purposes), the end result may be similar to that of giving shares to his or her children, as in the "Restriction on Share Transfers" section above. It is common for an agreement to provide that this type of transfer is acceptable as long as the transferring shareholder controls the holding company at all times. If voting control of the holding company were to change, then the transferring shareholder would be in default under the terms of the agreement.

Right of First Refusal

If an outsider (non-shareholder) wants to buy a shareholder's interest in the company, then that shareholder, before he or she can accept the outsider's offer, must give the other shareholders the opportunity to buy his or her shares for the same price and with the same terms and conditions. If the other shareholders do not want to buy at that price and under those conditions, then the selling shareholder is free to sell his or her shares to the outsider.

This provision gives shareholders the right to determine who their co-shareholders will be. By reducing the process to a financial decision, there is no need to explain thought processes or to comment on personality issues. If B and C do not want A to sell to an outsider, then they can buy A's shares themselves. If they cannot or will not spend the money to buy A's shares, then they are acknowledging that the outsider is an acceptable shareholder, or at least that having the outsider as a shareholder is less objectionable than spending the money to keep him or her out.

"Shotgun" Clause

When the "shotgun" trigger is pulled, in the context of a two shareholder corporation, there will soon be one shareholder. At the triggering moment, however, there is no way of knowing which one will remain. Suppose A wants to buy B's shares. Under the shotgun provision, he offers B, say, $200,000 for his shares. B now has two choices:

(a) He can accept A's offer of $200,000; or

(b) He can buy A's shares for $200,000.

At the end of the process, there will be just one shareholder, and someone will have received $200,000.

Note that there are only two choices for B. He cannot simply decline the offer and then go back to work as if nothing had happened.

The shotgun is designed primarily to prevent A from making a ridiculously low offer to B. The knowledge that B can turn the offer around makes sure that A's offer is reasonable.

Where A and B have dramatically different financial resources, the shotgun may still be unfair. A could offer B $100,000 for his shares if he knows that B is in financial difficulty and could not respond by coming up with $100,000 of his own to buy A's shares. There are always surprises, though, and many shotgun triggers have had unanticipated results.

Share Purchase on Death

An agreement will specify what happens in the event of the death of a shareholder, and will cover such details as:

- Who will buy the shares?

  (i) company,

  (ii) individuals,

  (iii) both (i) and (ii).

- At what price?
- Under what terms?

  (i) cash,

  (ii) payout over time.

- When will the purchase take place?

A primary purpose here is to ensure that the estate or heirs of the deceased shareholder do not remain shareholders in the company, unless this is intended, and that they receive fair value for the shares. It would be inappropriate to have to negotiate purchase price and terms, so as many details as possible are agreed upon in advance.

Use of Life Insurance

The company agrees to buy and maintain insurance on the life of each shareholder. It will pay premiums when due and will be the beneficiary of each policy.

The company also agrees to make appropriate elections when Capital Dividend Account credits created by the receipt of life insurance proceeds will be advantageous in a share repurchase arrangement.

With no reference to the CDA, it would be possible for the company to redeem shares at the appropriate price and comply with all other provisions of the agreement, while maintaining the CDA strictly for the benefit of surviving shareholders. Since there is no way of knowing in advance what the relative financial situations of the parties to the agreement (shareholders and corporation) will be at the time a shareholder dies, the significant benefit of the CDA should not simply be left to chance.

Disability

A shareholder agreement should address the question of disability in some detail. It is not essential that disability trigger a share purchase, nor is it essential that disability insurance funding be in place, but it is crucial for the basic issues to be addressed:

- How will disability be defined?
- What happens when the criteria are not met?

  (i) share repurchase,

  (ii) share re-organization,

  (iii) dividend payout.

- What happens when there is a full and complete recovery?
- How long does a disabled shareholder continue to receive salary?
- Does a disabled shareholder continue to receive bonuses?
- Can a disabled shareholder transfer shares to other family members?
- Who votes the shares of a disabled shareholder? Can a disabled shareholder have voting control?

In many ways, these issues are as important as those regarding a buy-out on death. Disability removes the shareholder from the role of active employee, but does not remove him or her as a shareholder, nor as a friend, family member, or colleague. Negotiating after the fact can be a traumatic process in which a "win–win" outcome is often impossible to achieve.

Restriction on Pledging Shares as Collateral

Typically, an agreement contains a clause prohibiting the assignment of shares as collateral for a loan. While this is understandable, and would be designed to avoid having a bank or other lender assume the position of a shareholder in the event of a default, it can appear somewhat idealistic. If a shareholder's principal (or sole) asset is his or her interest in the company, then it is unlikely that a prospective lender would be willing to ignore it. As so often happens, the real world calls for compromise.

Retirement of a Shareholder

In most cases, retirement is not specifically addressed in an agreement. Rather than trying to define retirement age and retirement income in advance, it may be more practical to have shareholders negotiate a deal at the appropriate time. With so many variables and so many changes in the concept of retirement, it may well be almost impossible to take any other approach.

Retirement itself involves discussion of succession and transition and so must be viewed along with holding companies, tax planning, shotgun clauses, estate freezing, and estate planning.

Default

Many shareholder agreements devote a significant amount of space to the concept of Default. What happens when a shareholder does not live up to the terms of the agreement, and what kind of remedies should be called for? Without these provisions, there may well be a tendency to seek remedies in a court of law, with all of the associated delays and expenses, so from this perspective it is advisable to have the possibility of default handled in some detail.

It should be remembered, however, that a shareholder agreement is essentially a contract of good faith, and that if an agreement attempts to address every conceivable eventuality, then its drafting and execution will take longer than anyone would want to spend, and the end result may be so cumbersome as to defeat the main purpose.

The Agreement as a Succession Planning Tool

A properly drafted shareholder agreement can address many essential components of a succession plan:

- Future share ownership can be specified in advance;

- If funded appropriately, a "fire sale" situation can be avoided, preserving optimum share values;

- Where an agreement includes family members, ownership of a business can remain within the family. In the event that children do not outlive their parents, it may be important for shares not to pass outside the family. A child's will, for example, might provide for shares to pass to a spouse in the event of death, so an agreement could provide for the spouse to receive the value of the shares rather than the shares themselves;

- Optimum tax treatment can be designed by providing for a combination of cross-purchase and corporate share repurchase to take advantage of available SBGE and CDA amounts where appropriate; and

- In a family business context, the founder of the business can inject into the agreement various provisions dealing with ongoing management, such as the hiring and firing of senior management, remuneration, dividend distributions, and so on. Experience has shown that when the second generation inherits a family business with an agreement in place, things tend to go more smoothly than if they were to try to come up with an agreement after the fact.

Control

In its simplest terms, control refers to the ability to cast the majority of the votes at a meeting of the board of directors.

While many business owners, both inside and outside a family business environment, are willing to discuss gradual ownership transition, even to transfer equity and growth potential to others, the idea of giving up control seems to be truly terrifying.

When structuring a shareholder agreement as part of a succession plan, voting control must be addressed at each step along the way. This is especially true when looking at buy-outs or share repurchases and redemptions.

If, for example, a retiring shareholder is having his or her shares redeemed by the company over a period of time, there will come a point when just one more share redeemed will result in a loss of voting control. If this is not planned for, then it will come as quite a shock.

As usual, there are two different viewpoints here:

(a) If shareholder V is selling his shares over time, he needs to have some element of control as long as the company still owes him a substantial sum of money;

(b) If shareholder P is running the company now that V has retired, then he or she does not want V interfering in board decisions or generally being a nuisance. The most important point to recognize when dealing with voting control is that it is a crucial issue, with lots of emotion attached to it, that must be factored into all the planning discussions and alternatives.

Flexibility

One thing all advisors know is that things will not turn out the way we thought. The business world is in such a state of rapid change that long-term plans must contain sufficient flexibility to be able to adapt when change occurs.

An agreement that calls for a share redemption using 100% of the Capital Dividend Account of the corporation will present problems if the arrangement is not "grandfathered". Similarly, an agreement based on the old 25% solution for stop-loss purposes will be less efficient in a 50% solution environment. At some point, the optimum solution may well involve a negotiated arrangement between the estate of the deceased and the surviving shareholders. The certainty of an agreement has to be tempered by the flexibility required for changing circumstances.

When we discuss business succession plans with a 50 year old business owner who would like to see his 23 year old son take over his position "one day", any agreement to be put into place between the current 50:50 shareholders will need to allow for that possibility. This is not a certainty, however, since the son may change his mind or may even have no ability in this area.

The major point to bear in mind here is that whenever we go through 40- or 50-year projections, it is essential that we build in "escape hatches" along the way, and add the flexibility that we know will be necessary.

Occasionally, clients may feel reluctant to plan at all, given the likelihood, or rather the certainty, of change. This is somewhat like refusing to leave home to drive to the office until you know for sure that all the traffic lights are green, that there are no accidents, no construction detours, no radar traps, and that there is a perfect parking space waiting. The important thing is to begin a plan, to recognize change and act accordingly. The alternative — waiting until "one day" when the conditions may be right — is a recipe for disaster, chaos, and expense.

C H A P T E R 8

Estate Freezing

An estate freeze is a process whereby capital assets whose continued growth creates escalating tax and succession concerns are exchanged for similar assets that are fixed in value.

Setting Objectives

As with all steps in the planning process, the starting point for a discussion of estate freezing begins with a review of the client's objectives. While the tax efficiency and sheer poetry of a finely executed estate freeze may be a desirable end result from the advisor's viewpoint, a freeze is, in reality, no more than one of the tools to be used to provide a solution to specific concerns expressed by the client.

Once the objectives of the client have been identified, however approximately, then it is appropriate to review those objectives and look at alternative methods of achieving them.

Why Freeze?

An estate freeze, whether total (rare nowadays) or partial, can be a useful way of moving toward the following objectives:

- Fixing capital gains tax liability at today's level;

- Passing asset growth to children without tax along the way;

- Facilitating a share purchase by an employee or group of employees;

- Ensuring that a family business can remain a family business;

- Maximizing access to the Small Business Gains Exemption;

- Crystallizing gains for the Small Business Gains Exemption;

- Allowing for an orderly, systematic redemption of shares following retirement, or in the event of total disability;

- Income splitting (beware the attribution rules); and

- Structuring a stream of dividend income to a retiring shareholder.

Alternatives

Suppose M Ltd. is owned 100% by M. At the age of 50, M is considering an estate freeze in order to save taxes (long-term) and facilitate business ownership transition.

In discussion with his advisors, M has agreed that he is too young to do a 100% freeze, and has decided to transfer 50% of the growth in value of M Ltd. to his two children, 25% to his wife, and 25% to himself.

There are several methods whereby M could achieve his objective, but we will concentrate here on the two most common methods:

Section 85 Rollover

M incorporates a holding company, Hco, and issues 25% of the common shares, all with nominal value (Hco has no assets and no income) to each of himself, his wife, and his children.

He then transfers his common shares of Mco to Hco in exchange for preferred shares. If Mco was worth $500,000, he would transfer them to Hco in exchange for redeemable, retractable preferred shares with a value of $500,000.

The "rollover" provision of section 85 allows for this transfer to be done without tax, as long as the value of the Hco preferred shares is equal to the value of the common shares of Mco. In addition, the ACB of the preferred shares should be equal to the ACB of the Mco common shares. In effect, any excess of the ACB of the Hco preferred shares over the ACB of the Mco common shares becomes a current capital gain.

M arranges for the preferred shares he receives from Hco to have a Fair Market Value of $500,000 and an ACB of $500,000. This gives M a capital gain of $500,000, to which he applies his Small Business Gains Exemption.

His preferred shares in Hco are fixed in value, since Hco can redeem them at any time for $500,000 (they are redeemable) and M could demand that they be redeemed for $500,000 (they are retractable).

Consequently, any future increase in the value of Mco, which is owned 100% by Hco, will be reflected in the common shares of Hco:

Duration	Value of Mco	Value of Hco preferreds	Value of Hco commons
5 years	$ 750,000	$ 500,000	$ 250,000
10 years	$1,500,000	$ 500,000	$1,000,000
20 years	$5,000,000	$ 500,000	$4,500,000

In this example, the value of the Hco commons will be divided equally among M, his wife, and the two children, but the share structure of Hco could have been arranged at the outset to provide any other ownership proportion. If M had decided to do a 100% freeze, passing all growth to the children, then his interest would remain at $500,000 throughout, and the Hco common shares could belong solely to the children.

From a tax perspective alone, a 100% freeze can be attractive:

Duration	Tax on M's death if 100% freeze	Tax on M's death if 75% freeze
5 years	0*	$ 12,500
10 years	0*	$ 50,000
20 years	0*	$225,000

If M and Mrs. M use a spousal rollover to defer tax until the second to die, then the tax numbers shown above could be deferred (assuming Mrs. M survives M).

Using a section 85 rollover, it is important to remember that M no longer owns Mco. He and the other family members own Hco, which in turn owns Mco. Any sale of shares hoping to benefit from SBGE treatment would have to be a sale of Hco shares, so it would be important to keep Hco "clean", with no other significant assets or investment funds or properties.

Section 86 Re-organization

Rather than create a new company for the purposes of a freeze, M might decide instead to simply re-organize the shares of Mco. He would return to Mco all of his shares, receiving in exchange preferred shares with the same value, and Mco would then issue new common shares for nominal consideration.

In all major respects, the rollover treatment is the same as for a section 85 rollover, simply without the use of a second corporation.

Where there are no other shareholders, and where no long-term investment diversification objectives are in sight, a section 86 re-organization can be somewhat simpler and more direct.

---

* SBGE used at time of rollover.

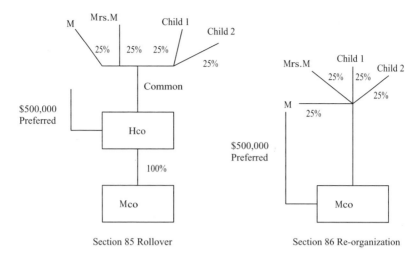

Section 85 Rollover   Section 86 Re-organization

As long as the children who receive common shares are not minors, there should be no application of the attribution rules.

Corporate Attribution Rules

Subsection 74.4(2) of the Act provides that if an individual transfers property to a corporation, and one of the reasons for the transfer is to reduce his or her taxable income in favour of a spouse or minor child, then he or she is deemed to receive interest at the prescribed rate.

This sub-section is not a concern in estate freezing as long as the corporation in question constitutes a small business corporation (i.e., a corporation having at least 90% of the fair market value of its assets used principally in an active business carried on primarily in Canada).

Retaining Real Estate

Suppose that, approaching age 65, Walter decides to retire. His children will continue to run the company, Wco, and will ultimately inherit the business outright. Meanwhile, however, Walter is looking for a business structure that will provide him with some income and some security.

For discussion purposes, assume that Wco Ltd. has a value of $3,000,000, of which $1,000,000 is represented by the land and building occupied by the business.

In this situation, Walter could incorporate a second company, Wco2 Ltd., then have Wco Ltd. transfer to the new company all assets of the business with the exception of the land and building, which remain in Wco.

Common shares of Wco2 will be owned by the children, preferred shares by Wco.

The completed structure would look as follows:

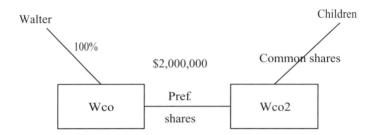

The assets of Wco, which is still owned 100% by Walter, consist of the land and building and $2,000,000 of preferred shares of Wco2, received in exchange for the business assets transferred.

This type of structure allows Walter's company to receive income (dividends on the preferred shares paid to Wco, and business rent paid to Wco by Wco2), and the land and building offer some security. Wco could pay income to Walter by way of salary or dividend, and could keep some money for investment.

Using Life Insurance Instead

Whenever extensive planning is undertaken with a view to reducing taxes payable on death, it is not uncommon to wonder, if it would not be a lot simpler just to buy a whole bunch of life insurance instead.

Alas, for those of us directly interested in the sale of bunches of life insurance, this is not normally a good alternative, and the costs of the planning and freezing are not necessarily many times the cost of buying life insurance.

If the sole objective of an estate freeze were to save, for example, $1,000,000 of tax on the death of the second to die of a husband and wife, then a good "fail-safe"check would be to compare the costs involved with cost of buying $1,000,000 of joint-second-to-die life insurance.

Of course, an estate freeze normally offers more advantages than tax deferral, especially when completed as part of a business succession plan, so the issue is not simply one of tax savings.

Life insurance does, in itself, bring other advantages, such as tax reduction through the Capital Dividend Account, the opportunity for creditor protection, and the potential for tax-sheltered savings.

In the vast majority of cases, life insurance would not be a substitute for an estate freeze, but should be included as part of the freeze, providing the best of both worlds.

Voting Control

As mentioned earlier, giving up future share value is not nearly as traumatic as giving up voting control. Normally, whether a freeze is completed via section 85 rollover or via section 86 re-organization, the preferred shares issued to the freezor carry voting control.

In the example of M receiving $500,000 of preferred shares in Mco, with common shares going to all family members, it might be structured so that preferred shares carry, say, 500 votes each, while common shares carry one vote each. As long as any preferred share is outstanding, it outvotes the common shares. It could also be arranged that the preferred shares are voting shares only in the hands of the original holder, ceasing to have any votes once they pass to an estate or heir. This would minimize concerns for children working in the family business who would not want to be outvoted by inactive siblings.

Reversing a Freeze

Reversing an estate freeze is a complex process, and should be viewed as a last resort. It does happen, however, that family relationships deteriorate or that some other life-changing event means that the freeze has to be undone.

If the growth (common) shares were issued to a trust for the children, then this might provide more flexibility, but ideally, this could be taken one step further if a grandparent rather than a parent is the settlor of the trust.

In M's example earlier, if M's mother or father had settled a trust to hold the common shares of Mco, then M could be included as a contingent beneficiary of the trust, and would, under specified circumstances, be able to receive a distribution of common shares from the trust, effectively removing the effects of the freeze.

Where it is not possible to actually reverse a freeze, it may be possible to limit the effects of the freeze by completing a second freeze, this time giving the children preferred shares and the parents new common shares.

Points to Consider

- If a shareholder completes a freeze by giving shares to children, the children actually own the shares. As shareholders, the children should be parties to a shareholder agreement;

- If a discretionary trust is used to hold shares for future distribution to the children, then the parents/trustees have up to 21 years to decide who should become a shareholder;

- The divorce, death, bankruptcy, or incapacity of a child might cause a triggering event under a shareholder agreement, but would have no structural or tax impact if the shares were held by a discretionary trust;

- An estate freeze can fix the amount of capital gains tax. Generally, it does not make the tax go away, nor does it provide the means to pay the tax. Life insurance can and should be an integral part of the planning process;

- Involving all children equally as shareholders is not necessarily an equitable solution. The survival needs of the business must be balanced with the need for equality among children; and

- An estate freeze is not a business succession plan, but rather a part of the plan. It has to be consistent with the original objectives of the founding shareholder or shareholders.

CHAPTER 9

Assessing Personal Priorities

When an individual prepares to embark upon the estate/succession planning process, the primary task is to make sure that personal priorities are quite clearly established. In the absence of this clarity, it is all too easy to implement plans that may have "seemed like a good idea at the time" but which, in fact, are counter-productive in some way.

Of course, when it comes to a discussion of personal priorities, the number of available options and combinations is probably infinite, but there are some principal priorities which need to be assessed and incorporated into plans.

Minimizing Taxes

The desire to minimize taxes is basic, and is recognized as a fundamental component of the planning process. The CCRA and the courts draw a distinction between reducing or avoiding taxes (OK) and evading taxes (not OK) and, generally speaking, there is lots of room to manoeuvre without crossing the legal/illegal line.

If a client's primary objective is really to minimize taxes, then the answer is simple: do not earn income.

This probably seems a little impractical, so the client will need to revise the objective, and focus on minimizing taxes while earning the same income.

In the context of succession planning, the desire to minimize taxes can easily be met by leaving everything to a surviving spouse. This would have several impacts:

(a) No capital gains tax would be paid;

(b) The surviving spouse would be the owner of the shares. Assuming the spouse is not directly involved in running the business, then his or her objectives (receiving bonus or dividend income) might be in serious conflict with those of whoever is actually running the business;

(c) Although no tax would be paid, the tax would be deferred rather than avoided. It will still be payable at some future date; and

(d) If the person running the business (child, key employee, sibling, or whoever else could do the job) has no share interest, then planning for the next step in the succession process is almost impossible. All too often, the next step will be deferred until the death of the spouse who inherited the shares.

A recent, and admittedly extreme, example of this type of situation involved a widow in her 80s who had inherited from her husband all of the shares of an operating company of significant value. The company was run by two sons, in their 50s, who were not able to address the issue of succession planning for themselves. At the point in time where they would normally be thinking of bringing their children into the business, perhaps via a partial freeze, they could do nothing. Their mother could have facilitated, but chose not to.

In the short-term, this was an effective tax plan, but in the big picture, it was a total disaster. Minimizing taxes can be an attractive objective, but it has to be put in its proper perspective.

Maximizing Personal Freedom

This is an area which tends to receive less than its due share of attention, as many clients try to squeeze their definition of personal freedom into the confines of a completed plan, rather than using that definition as the starting point.

If, for example, Doris, a retired computer consultant who has $2,000,000 in inherited wealth (from her father) invested in various stocks, whether or not this contributes to her sense of freedom depends in large part on her risk tolerance. She will need to reconcile the opportunity to earn a higher rate of return with the desire for some form of security. There is no freedom in the wealth if she worries about its safety.

Similarly, the sale of a business to a child, key employee, or outsider can be a source of frustration or a source of freedom, depending on the approach.

If Bill wants to sell his business for $1,500,000 and his "for sale" sign generates two offers, his choice will not be dictated by price alone:

(a) He receives an offer for $1,500,000, conditional upon his remaining an active employee for two years, with $500,000 paid up front (to utilize the SBGE) and the balance to be paid over a five-year period; and

(b) He receives an offer of $1,200,000 cash, with no conditions attached. Offer (b) is clearly more attractive if Bill is looking for freedom. The extra money in (a) is not a good trade-off.

In a family business environment, the founding shareholder may well decide to freeze his shares and receive dividend income in Hawaii or the Caribbean, leaving management and control of the company to his children, rather than trying to go through the mechanics of a financed sale. If he or she is confident in the children's ability to keep the company healthy, this could be a stress-free solution. If not, he or she would be better advised to try for a sale, even if he or she has to accept less than optimum price.

The point is that we should not confuse money with freedom. Freedom is as difficult to define as success, and there are probably as many definitions as there are clients.

In the planning process, we need to know in advance how important this is for any particular client. A plan that scores six out of 10 on the tax scale and 10 out of 10 on the freedom scale may be a better solution than one with more tax efficiency.

Passing Wealth to Future Generations

When dealing with the concept of wealth and its movement to future generations, there are generally two extreme points of view:

(a) "I had to work hard for everything I have. My children can do the same."

(b) "It is important for me to give my children every financial advantage I can, even if it means that I have to make sacrifices in terms of current income."

Most clients have a view somewhere in between the two extremes.

It is not uncommon for owners of family businesses to want to subordinate all other objectives in an attempt to keep the family business going for one or two more generations.

This view depends in part on the children themselves, of course. If children are irresponsible spendthrifts with no discernible work ethic, then that will influence any succession planning initiatives.

The key is that, as advisors, we should not assume, but rather make a specific effort to uncover the priorities involved.

Passing Wealth to Charities

Many successful business owners are actively involved in their communities, regularly contributing both time and money to various charitable organizations. Others are so consumed by the everyday demands of the business that every conceivable minute and every potential dollar are accounted for many times over.

During the succession planning process, a spotlight is shone on the potential tax liability faced by a client's estate, and the concept of "social capital" is often introduced.

Scott Fithian, president of Legacy Advisory Associates in Boston, talks of "social capital" as the taxes a client pays or the charitable bequests a client makes. If the client's philanthropic interests coincide exactly with the expenditure patterns of the federal and provincial governments, then all he or she needs to do is pay taxes. If, on the other hand, the client has specific philanthropic intent, or even if he or she disagrees with the way the government spends its tax revenues, then the client has the opportunity to decide how this particular block of "social capital" should be spent.

It is important at this stage to recognize that the "how to" is not an issue, and that we need to focus on the "what". If a client decides that he or she would rather divide wealth between beneficiaries and charities than between beneficiaries and government, then that decision becomes part of the motivation behind the planning process.

The new rules allowing an individual to donate public company shares to a charity, and include only 25% of the capital gain in income instead of the usual 50%, provide a strong incentive to demonstrate philanthropy during lifetime. While not generally applicable to the business succession process, this particular provision does allow for some creativity, using tax savings triggered by a donation of publicly traded stock to shelter other income in that year, other income which could result from intra-family share transfers in the family business.

Family Harmony

Perhaps there is no more demanding task than trying to pass business ownership from one generation to another, while maintaining family harmony. In assessing the importance of this for any particular client, it is helpful, where possible, to speak to all family members involved.

While the founder of a family business may often (but not always) be willing to discuss succession plans with his wife, or with any child or children directly involved in the business, it is unusual for the entire family to discuss this delicate subject together.

A key leadership role for the advisor is to promote such a family discussion, perhaps even offering to "mediate" such a discussion and take notes.

The simple truth is that most people would rather not discuss the prospect of their own mortality, and the family business environment makes this even more difficult.

If family harmony is a key issue for a client, then the plans must be discussed with other family members. Equalization of inheritances may be a crucial factor, leaving non-business assets to children not involved in the business, sometimes using life insurance to create cash for the equalization process.

On occasion, a client may be reluctant to begin any serious succession planning because he or she does not want to disturb family harmony. Where a business is owned 50:50 by brothers, for example, then a brother with three or four children may have a completely different view than his brother with no children or with one child who has no interest whatsoever in the business. Walking on egg-shells becomes the order of the day — not a conventional succession planning concept, admittedly, but a crucial one in this context. The technical tools of succession planning have little to offer unless the family dynamics say that it is safe to proceed.

Shelter From Business Risk

A successful small business is almost invariably the result of many years of hard work, of personal and financial sacrifices, and perhaps even a little luck along the way.

When the time comes to begin thinking of succession planning, some of the thoughts running through the business owner's mind will include:

- At last there may be a big "payday";

- No one else could possibly run the business as well as I did;

- It will be nice to hand over the day-to-day worries to someone else;

- What if the business fails?; and

- I can always keep an eye on things.

At times, shelter from business risk becomes a vital consideration. A retiring shareholder may not want to have any ongoing dependence on the success of the business. If there is debt, then it has to be secured. If there are personal guarantees in place, they have to be released.

It should be remembered that the obsession and dedication to a single purpose, probably a reason for the success of the business, can become a liability in retirement. As long as money is at risk, then there may in effect be no retirement. We need to know where each particular client fits.

The Advisor's Role

In assessing personal priorities, the role of the advisor is not to know the answers or to have everything at their fingertips, but to know the questions.

With many of these questions, the client will not know the answer. The question has probably never been considered before. Indeed, when the "right" kind of question is asked, two people learn the answers for the first time: the advisor and the client.

The most valuable function of the advisor is to be a guide through the process of determining personal priorities and objectives. Anyone can design an answer or a solution. The real art consists of knowing the questions.

CHAPTER **10**

Tax Planning
Approaches

A n exhaustive analysis of tax planning is beyond the scope of this publication, but certain general principles should be kept in mind during the planning process.

Tax Planning Alternatives

Tax avoidance is legal and socially acceptable. Tax evasion is not. Among the list of avoidance mechanisms are alternatives such as:

- Defer receipt of recognition of income. Capital gains "rollover" to a spouse is an example of income deferral;

- Arrange to take advantage of all exemptions. The SBGE is the most significant example and most business owners will go to considerable trouble and expense to make sure it does not get away;

- Arrange to receive income in its most tax efficient form. If earned income and interest income are taxed at 40%, capital gains at 20% and dividends at 25%, then there would normally be a preference for capital gains. This will have an impact on how a shareholder agreement is structured or on how a sale to an outsider is put together;

- Look for income that will not be taxed, or whose exposure to tax can be controlled. Generally speaking, income earned in a life insurance policy is not taxable as long as it remains inside the policy. This provides a long-term tax shelter. Indeed, if it is simply considered capital, the death benefit ultimately payable from the policy is received tax free, even though it may consist of policyholder payments plus investment earnings. Life insurance companies pay a 15% Investment Income Tax on behalf of policyholders, so there is some element of taxation during the accumulation stages;

- Try to have income taxed where the burden will be the lightest. Income received by a CCPC/QSBC will be taxed at around 20% on the first $200,000. Income splitting with family members used to be popular, but recent legislative changes have made this difficult for minor children. For adult children, more opportunity exists, although it would still not be appropriate to pay a 20-year old university student $50,000 a year just to sweep the company parking lot during summer vacation;

- Arrange for future capital growth to take place in the hands of a future generation. The classic "estate freeze" allows for future growth to occur in the hands of children or grandchildren. Whichever method is used in a given situation, it should be used because it fits with personal priorities and is tax effective, not simply because it is tax effective.

United States Citizens

The Canadian *Income Tax Act* basically imposes a duty for paying tax on all who live in Canada, regardless of citizenship.

The United States, however, has a dramatically different view, requiring all its citizens to pay United States taxes, regardless of where they live.

For many clients, this introduces many new obstacles to the planning process and requires highly specialized advice.

The major problem areas, of course, revolve around estate tax and income tax, and the following brief references are meant only to indicate the potential scope of the problem.

Estate Tax Considerations

(i) United States citizens are required to pay estate taxes on all of their worldwide assets. A basic exemption of $2,000,000 is available. As an example, a United States citizen with a $10,000,000 estate, of which the U.S. property consists only of a $200,000 condominium in Phoenix, will be eligible for a basic $2,000,000 exemption and will be liable for estate tax of several million dollars.

If the client is also a Canadian citizen, nothing changes. U.S. citizenship carries with it these tax issues, regardless of what other citizenships may be held. Consequently, if an advisor asks a client if he or she is a Canadian citizen, an answer in the affirmative is not necessarily an "all clear" signal. We need to ask what other citizenships are held.

The newly ratified U.S.–Canada Protocol provides some relief from the possibility of double taxation, but the relief is not complete.

(ii) If the individual in the example above were a non-U.S. citizen, not living in the United States, then his or her death would still result in estate tax liability in the U.S. His or her only U.S. asset is the $200,000 Phoenix condo, but the basic exemption is pro-rated according to the percentage of assets in the United States. His or her worldwide estate is worth $10,000,000 and the condo is worth $200,000, so the estate tax exemption is $625,000 (since the exemption was not raised for non-resident aliens) × $200,000/$10,000,000 = $12,500 and the client's estate would expect a significant tax bill (rates range from 18% to 45%).

Recently enacted legislation aims for repeal of the U.S. Estate Tax legislation. In 2010, estate tax will cease to exist. It will, however, be reinstated in 2011 unless further legislation is forthcoming, under an unusual "sunset clause". To make matters worse, the reinstatement takes place at 2001 levels, prior to the increase in exemption amounts and the reduction in top rates from 55% to

45%. (It is estimated that estate tax repeal would result in a loss of US$289 billion in government revenue over the next 10 years.)

Income Tax Considerations

If a client is a U.S. citizen (regardless of other citizenships held), then great care must be exercised in the succession planning process.

If, for example, a client transfers shares to an adult child and triggers a $500,000 capital gain, the SBGE will look after the Canadian tax liability, but there is no corresponding exemption in the United States.

Similarly, estate freezing by means of a section 85 "rollover" has no U.S. counterpart and may produce costly and unintended results.

Gift Tax

To complicate matters even more, the United States also imposes a gift tax of 18% to 55% (rates used to be tied to the estate tax rates, but were "disconnected" in the estate tax revision process) on a donor who makes gifts to any person in excess of $12,000, or to a non-U.S. spouse of over $120,000.

If gift tax is triggered by a U.S. citizen resident in Canada, there is no tax credit in Canada.

A lifetime exemption of $1,000,000 exists for the gift tax. The proposed abolition of estate tax is not accompanied by the abolition of gift tax.

The area of Canada/U.S. taxation is becoming increasingly complex and specialized. With the increased incidence of people moving between the two countries, it is essential to make sure that a simple oversight cannot destroy plans made. Many clients moved to Canada from the United States when they were young children and may not even be aware of their citizenship status.

CHAPTER 11

Valuation Issues

Whenever shares or assets are moved around, special attention must be paid to the valuation of those assets.

Fair Market Value

As a general rule, a transaction is assumed to have taken place at Fair Market Value (FMV). If A sells land to B for $200,000, then $200,000 is assumed to be the FMV of the property. Or at least that is the case if A and B are not related and therefore deal with each other "at arm's length". Logically, A would not sell the land for $200,000 if he or she thought it was worth more than that, and B would not pay $200,000 if he or she thought it was worth less than that. A nice, simple concept.

But what if A and B are related? Then A might be willing to sell the land to B, his son, for $100,000. This would not be a FMV transaction, and would take place on a "non-arm's length" basis.

The *Income Tax Act* makes numerous references to "arm's length" and "non-arm's length", and offers this definition: "Related persons shall be deemed not to deal with each other at arm's length" (251(1)) and then "related persons" are defined as "Individuals connected by blood relationship, marriage or adoption" (251(2)(a)).

The "non-arm's length" concept is also extended to corporations and their shareholders and to corporations dealing with other corporations, and much has been written about the finer points of deciding whether or not a non-arm's length relationship exists between parties to a transaction.

The basic assumption is that arm's length parties deal at Fair Market Value and non-arm's length parties would prefer not to.

For tax purposes, the reference point is Fair Market Value, but this term is not defined in the Act, although it is mentioned in several places. It is generally agreed that, in order for a transaction to take place, it should involve the following components:

- A willing seller (i.e., no "fire sale");

- A willing buyer;

- An open and unrestricted market;

- Seller and buyer must be in possession of all relevant facts (e.g., no "hidden" development permits, no threatened lawsuits, no impending "killer" competition);

- There must be no compulsion to act; and

- Value must be expressed in terms of money.

When buyer and seller are related, it is essential that an uninvolved third party provide guidance as to valuation.

As an example, assume that L, the owner of Lco, plans to "freeze" his share value at its current level, giving future growth to his children. He believes the current value of Lco is $2,000,000, and the resulting structure is as follows:

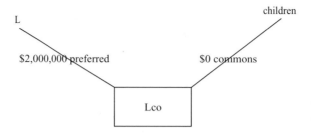

If, however, the value of the company were really $3,000,000, then the transaction should have taken place at this level. Since L only took back preferred shares of $2,000,000, then the structure will be

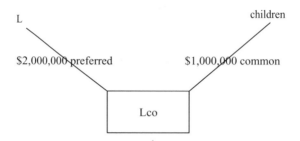

L will be considered to have made a gift of $1,000,000 of common shares to his children, resulting in an additional capital gain to him. In addition, the children will still be considered to have an ACB of $0 for the shares, so that gain may ultimately be taxed twice.

This situation can be avoided by having a qualified professional value the business.

The Valuation Process

The valuator of a privately held corporation faces a difficult task. The usual indicators of net income, sustainable net income, goodwill and so on will all help, but there is often an undefinable "something" that makes all the difference. Nevertheless, a valuator will normally begin by reviewing recent financial statements, comparing revenues and profits with those of similar businesses, looking for special "niche" values and uniqueness, identifying non-business assets, reviewing credit history and so on.

To some extent, it is possible to look for industry averages and guidelines. If, for example, insurance agencies are typically valued at one time gross commission income, then that is a relatively simple process. Most small businesses manage to avoid the simple definitions, however, and the valuation process becomes as much an art as a science.

Differing Views of Value

Most business owners have a good idea of what their business is worth, or, at least, they know how big a cheque it would take for them to walk away, which is close to knowing, but not quite the same thing.

There are exceptions, however, and discussions of value can be a precarious, even dangerous part of the planning process. For example, XYZ Co. Ltd. might earn profits of $40,000 to $50,000 annually, yet the owner insists it has a value of $5,000,000. The "big breakthrough" will be here any time soon, and they would not sell it for less than $5,000,000. At the other end of the spectrum, a company earning $800,000 annually is, according to its owner, worth no more than $1,500,000 to $2,000,000, since the income level is an anomaly and will settle down once the market for the product/service offered becomes more realistic.

The key is to rationalize and document the valuation approach taken. Files that contain only numbers and spreadsheets would be much more helpful if they also contained a written summary of the valuation methods considered. Bear in mind that the methods used may not be re-visited for many years, long after the parties involved have forgotten what conversations or arguments took place at the time.

Inevitably, different views of the value of a small business will be held by different parties:

- The vendor will usually think the value should be higher;

- The purchaser usually thinks it should be lower;

- The taxation authorities look for higher values;

- Children who inherit non-business assets usually believe that the shares inherited by their siblings have a much greater value; and

- Banks and other lenders will normally take a conservative view of value.

To use a real estate analogy, when a house on their street is sold, people are often interested in finding out the selling price, then comparing it with what they think is the value of their own. This is human nature, and the sale of shares in a small business is really a similar event. Everyone has a definite opinion, often unimpeded by the facts.

Tax Considerations

Section 69 of the Act provides in part that

(a) If a taxpayer acquires anything from someone with whom he does not deal at arm's length, he is deemed to have acquired it at Fair Market Value;

(b) If a taxpayer sells anything to someone with whom he does not deal at arm's length, he is deemed to have sold it at Fair Market Value; and

(c) If a taxpayer inherits anything he is deemed to have acquired it for its Fair Market Value.

The implication of this section can be devastating if no attention is paid to the valuation question.

If, for example, A sells property to B, his son, they are deemed to be dealing on a non-arm's length basis. If A sells B property with a FMV of $150,000 for $100,000, then:

- A is deemed to have received $150,000; and

- B is deemed to have paid only $100,000.

This "one way" adjustment means that, in B's hands, the property's eventual increase in value from $100,000 to $150,000 will be a taxable capital gain, even though that $50,000 has already been taxed in A's hands.

Where parties to a transaction do not deal with each other at arm's length, an objective valuation is crucial. Where they do deal at arm's length, an objective valuation is still valuable, so that each party is comfortable with the fairness of the transaction.

The Family Farm

Special Considerations

W hen it comes to succession planning, the family farm should be treated like any other business, going through the same planning and discussion processes.

In reality, the situation is much more difficult than with any other type of business, for such reasons as:

- The family home is usually located on the farm. How many business owners would want to retire if it meant they had to move out of their home?

- Farming is capital intensive, which may tend to scare away successor owners;

- Most farm families tend to have the vast majority of their net worth tied up in the farm itself;

- Usually, all of the children work on the family farm while growing up. This creates a strong emotional bond with the farm, but may also imply an element of ownership or entitlement that cannot fit within a conventional succession plan; and

- Farming can be a 24-hour a day occupation and there is often little distinction between business and personal interests. In many instances, there are no personal interests outside the farm.

The Small Business Gains Exemption

The $500,000 exemption is available to an individual taxpayer who sells farm property, including:

- Land and buildings used in the business of farming;

- Eligible capital property used in the business of farming (farm quotas, for example);

- Shares of a Family Farm Corporation; and

- Interest in a Family Farm Corporation.

Special criteria to be met in order for the property to qualify:

- The individual must have owned the property for at least 24 months; and

- Gross revenue from the farming business exceeded income from all other sources in at least two years.

This second point means that hobby farms will not qualify.

In order for shares of a Family Farm Corporation to qualify, the company must meet the same test as the QSBC outlined earlier, with at least 90% of its assets used at the time of disposition in earning income from farming, and 50% over a 24 month period ending prior to the sale.

If shares of a Family Farm Corporation qualify for the exemption, then "crystallizing" the gain might be advised, since the corporation could start to build up investment assets or non-farming assets and lose its ability to qualify in the future.

This provision allows an individual farm owner to transfer property to children, triggering $500,000 of gain to be sheltered by the exemption, and providing the children who receive the shares with a collective $500,000 of Adjusted Cost Base.

From this point of view, the succession planning process for a family farm may look quite similar to that of any other business, but then some special tax provisions provide more flexibility and opportunity.

The Family Farm Rollover

The family farm is a unique business structure in Canada. It is the only one eligible for transfer to the next generation without current tax liability, regardless of amount.

In order to qualify for this special "rollover", the farm property must:

1. Be located in Canada; and

2. Be used principally in the business of farming carried on regularly and continuously by the taxpayer, his or her spouse or any child.

Details of the qualification process are outlined in Interpretation Bulletin IT-268R4, and, much of the discussion revolves around the term "principally", commonly taken to mean more than 50%. In turn, this can mean that more than 50% of the asset is used in the business of farming, or that the entire asset is used more than 50% of the time in the business of farming.

If the farm property itself qualifies for the rollover, then it may be transferred to a child on a tax-deferred basis, and in this context there is an extended definition of the term "child", which includes:

- A child of the taxpayer;

- A child of the taxpayer's spouse;

- A grandchild of the taxpayer;

- A great-grandchild of the taxpayer;

- An adopted child;

- A child's spouse; and

- A person who, at any time prior to age 19 was wholly dependent on and under the custody and control of the taxpayer.

A taxpayer who owns and farms qualifying farm property, or who owns shares of a Family Farm Corporation or an interest in a Family Farm Partnership, has the flexibility to set up a succession plan in any way he or she sees fit without issue of taxes becoming an obstacle. Although it should be noted that farm inventory can only be transferred to a child at fair market value, unless the transfer is a consequence of the death of the transferor.

Suppose F, a farmer, transfers his farm property to his four children. The farm has a value of $2,000,000 and an ACB of $100,000. Using the rollover provisions, each child will receive farm property of $500,000, with an ACB of $25,000. The children would eventually be able to transfer any or all of the farm property to their children, and so on, with no incidence of tax along the way.

Tax Saving vs. Tax Deferral

If a family farm remains a family farm indefinitely, and if each successive generation farms the property actively, then tax is postponed indefinitely.

There is, however, a significant difference between tax saving and tax deferral. The Family Farm Rollover, just like a spousal rollover, is a means of deferring tax. The Small Business Gains Exemption, however, is a means of saving tax, and should not be overlooked when considering succession planning for a family farm.

In the above example, F transferred farm property to his four children equally. If he had, at the same time, decided to take advantage of the SBGE, then each child could have received the same $500,000 in property, but with an ACB of $150,000 each, instead of just $25,000.

Each of the four children would then be able to access his or her own $500,000 SBGE (assuming continuing qualification) at some future time.

If, one day, the farm were to be sold to an outsider, then the SBGE amounts which had been used to increase ACB would result in very significant tax savings ($100,000 per owner over the years) compared with the Family Farm Rollover, whose tax deferral comes to an end with a resounding crash when the sale day arrives.

While a client's intention to retain a Family Farm as a Family Farm indefinitely may be clear and sincere, there is, of course, no way of knowing if this will happen. Utilizing the $500,000 exemption wherever possible is a sound strategy in most situations.

Consulting with Stakeholders

I
n some instances, the process of succession planning is completed after many long, sometimes tedious, sessions with various legal and financial advisors. At the end of the process, the outside world sees little difference, and life goes on the way it should.

With many small businesses, however, and especially with family businesses, the planning process has to involve other parties if it is to avoid major obstacles and pitfalls. The very loyalties and eccentricities that act as the glue in the structure of a family business can melt away quickly when communication with stakeholders breaks down or is ignored.

Stakeholders would include anyone for whom the continuing ability of the business to survive and prosper is important:

Other Shareholders

Other shareholders have an obvious and direct interest in the succession process. Their rights and obligations are typically contained in the Articles of Incorporation and in any signed shareholder's agreement. The ability to move shares around normally requires the permission of other shareholders, so it is natural for advance notice to be given. Much more than mere notice should be involved, however, and this should go as far as active consultation. In a family-owned business, family members typically discuss all aspects of the business on a regular basis, but where a business involves two different "branches" of the family, fireworks can result. As an example, consider Smith Bros. Consulting Ltd. The company is owned 50:50 by two brothers, Alan and Edward. To recognize differing investment philosophies and priorities, each formed a holding company ten years ago, so the structure is now:

They have a shareholder agreement in place, but it enforces no restriction on transferring shares of either holding company as long as control remains within the family.

Accordingly, Alan, now 60 years old, is planning on retiring, and wants to do a "freeze" in favour of his son Philip and his daughter Ellen, who will each own 50% of the growth shares of Alco.

Edward, at age 55, has not really been considering retirement, but he does not like Phillip or Ellen and rather than face trying to develop a working relationship with them, has decided to retire and freeze his shares of Edco in favour of his son Jim. Unfortunately, Jim is much more interested in personal status and golf than he is in the future of Smith Bros. He will see this as an opportunity to spend even more time of the golf course "entertaining" clients.

It becomes clear that Smith Bros. will not thrive with Philip, Ellen and Jim in charge. On a 50:50 basis, Jim can thwart any business plans Philip and Ellen might bring to the table. Edward is uneasy about handing control over to Jim, but feels it is his right to do whatever he wants to with his shares of Edco, just as Alan does with Alco. This is a recipe for disaster.

Alan and Edward need to discuss their plans with each other, and not simply announce their plans. Perhaps Philip and Ellen should run the company in its entirety, organizing some kind of buy out of Edco to allow Edward to retire without having to involve Jim in the process.

Even in a business with many shareholders, the minority shareholders should be consulted during the process. They may come up with better alternatives than the ones being considered, and, like most people, will tend to support more enthusiastically plans into which they have had some input.

Whatever difficulties shareholders believe might be created by discussing plans in advance with other shareholders, the risks of not discussing them are significantly greater.

Employees

It is obvious that employees play a key role in the ongoing success of a business. While employees' skills can be replaced, the special contributions of senior, long-term employees go far beyond the physical skills provided.

Any employee "grapevine" system worthy of the name will always know when ownership discussions are under way, and, in the absence of official information will usually imagine all kinds of unpleasant possibilities.

In addition, key employees are typically the best ambassadors for a business and can offer real help in the transition process.

Again, it should be emphasized that consulting with key employees is not the same as simply informing them of decisions already made. If they qualify as stakeholders, then they should be involved.

Family Members

It is said that one of the loneliest jobs in the world is to be the President/CEO/CFO/sole shareholder of a small business. More often than not, there is no one with whom he or she is able to discuss problems, concerns, or even opportunities. Over time, the sole shareholder becomes accustomed to the situation, so that eventually, when he or she wants to make succession plans, he or she is reluctant to involve other family members. It is essential that family members be involved in the discussions, whether as a sounding board, a source of alternative ideas, or as confirmation of the business owner's thought processes to date.

A function of the business owner's advisors is to ensure that family members are involved, or at least informed, by the owner as matters progress. There may be some element of discomfort here on the owner's part, but there is simply no compelling reason for him or her to keep everything locked away inside until everything is neatly organized and completed. The process can be sufficiently stress-inducing without feeling that there's no one to turn to for understanding.

Suppliers

There is certainly no shortage of change in the business world today. Every page of the business section of every major newspaper has details of a business restructuring or change in ownership or amalgamation. People who have a special relationship with the business do not want to receive their information on that business from the press. When making significant changes to a business in terms of ownership or management, it makes good sense to keep key suppliers informed. They may be able to contribute some ideas to the process, but most importantly they would then be receiving reliable information rather than whatever version is being circulated via the grapevine. Suppliers typically attach significant importance to continuity in contacts and relationships, so for a smooth transition it is crucial for all to be informed along the way.

Customers

Many customers view themselves as partners in the success of a business. A customer who would refer a new customer to a business is an integral part of the business. Of course, it would be impractical and counter-productive to try to contact all customers, but key customers are simply too important to leave out of the information loop. If the process is handled with care, key customers can take an active interest in ensuring that the business not only survives but flourishes under new ownership. Many second and third generation business owners have learned to value the advice and counsel provided by customers who used to deal with their parents or grandparents.

Lenders

Relationships with lenders can be fragile at times. If a retiring shareholder was always the one who dealt with the bank, then his retirement may well cause some consternation on the part of the lender. Over and above contractual obligations, personal relationships are vitally important, and the relationship with a lender who has watched the business grow and prosper over the years is one to be protected.

Advisors

It is easy to assume that, as advisors are actively involved in the planning process, they will always be aware of changes, challenges, and opportunities. The fact remains, however, that advisors do get left out, for a variety of reasons, such as:

- The lawyer is seen as someone who is valuable only when it is time to draft agreements. Until that point, there is no need to involve the legal advisor;

- The insurance advisor provides a specific commodity to solve a specific problem or concern. Meanwhile, he or she has no real role to play; and

- The accounting advisor keeps financial statements up to date, returns filed and so on. There is no need for that right now.

These reasons may have no real validity, but if the client does not see the value of the team approach to succession planning, then one or more of the advisors will be left out. As advisors, many of us have been in the position of being presented with a new plan, investment, or business development idea worked out by the client and one of his or her other advisors. At that point, we can always see where some improvement could have been made along the way, but is it too late to offer suggestions? Would it be seen as objective advice, or as a criticism of the plan developed without our input?

The point to be made here is that the succession planning process has to be a team effort involving input from various disciplines and from customers and employees as well as owners and advisors. The reason that the business survival rate from one generation to the next is about one third is not that the product or service provided by the business suddenly becomes inferior or undesirable in some way. Much more likely is that the various stakeholders in the business are not all involved and they eventually begin to go off in different directions. The same energies are involved, they are just not working together, and this can be resolved by a serious effort to communicate.

How to Get Started

Identifying Key Motivators

I t is too easy to assume that everyone has the same objectives:

- Saving taxes, either now or later;
- Leaving a meaningful legacy; and
- Ensuring family harmony.

115

In reality, there are a multitude of objectives that are rarely expressed formally, in addition to the above three, but the advisor will never get to help the client identify objectives unless he or she can first identify the key motivators of a particular client.

Whether the client is wealthy or of average means, whether he or she is the owner of a large corporation or of a basement operation, the key to initiating the planning process is to find what "drives" the client.

Key motivators can be almost anything that is important to the client, but commonly include such potential items as:

- A desire to "win". This might be a search for victory over the tax man, over a competitor, or even over a parent who never thought he or she would succeed in business;

- A desire to see the next generation (and the next after that) experience even more success;

- A desire to be "fair", to pay the fair share of taxes, to treat heirs equally as much as possible;

- A desire to make "clever" business decisions, paying more attention to them than to the emotional and philosophical aspects of the planning process;

- A desire to "make a difference" in society, perhaps by an expansion of a university or hospital, or by providing a local park with a tennis court or fishing pier. Bigger goals require extra energy, but are no less significant as motivators;

- A desire to continue to provide employees with the opportunity to make a good living;

- A desire to work for as long as possible, to "wear out rather than rust out"; and

- A desire to protect heirs from the temptations presented by inherited wealth. This is just a sample list of key motivators, of course, and a complete listing would in all likelihood consist of hundreds of items.

The motivators you can identify for a particular client will indicate how the planning process should begin. Note that none of the above listed items are measurable in dollars, nor are they a commodity to be delivered to the client. The only way to uncover the motivators is to ask questions that encourage a client to talk rather than to simply convey information. A question like "How do you feel about making your children wealthy?" will yield more information than "How much money do you want to leave to your children?"

Motivators are feelings, not facts, so we have to make room in our "fact finding" for a discussion about how the client feels about various issues.

There is little point in spending time analyzing data, doing projections and calculations to demonstrate that leaving the business to his or her children will result in a $2,000,000 tax liability in a business owner's estate, only to discover later on that he or she feels the children should look after that themselves as their contribution to the purchase price. A problem is only a problem if it is important to that particular client. If we mis-read the client, then the beauty, symmetry, and sheer poetry of a solution we design is wasted.

Assembling Information

The actual process of gathering information in order to complete the succession planning process can involve looking forward to making progress, or it can be a source of extreme discomfort. Some people are good record-keepers, and some avoid any kind of detail work at all costs.

Most advisors have some form of fact-finder or questionnaire they use in order to collect information and to make sure that nothing is overlooked, and, as long as it gets the job done, all will be well and good.

It is possible, though, and often preferable, to have "big picture" discussions with clients, getting a clear idea of priorities and concerns, and then to request permission to obtain various financial details from the client's accountant. Many clients do not normally concern themselves with all of the details and would, in all likelihood, prefer not to have to try to remember them. If an objective is to make the succession planning process as simple as possible, then we need to involve the client directly only in those discussions and decisions that require his or her personal input.

Looking at Available Resources

The disciplines involved in the succession planning process routinely include:

- Accounting
- Law
- Life & disability insurance

- Mutual funds & other investments

- Tax

If one or more of these disciplines is already available to the client, it is questionable whether anything positive is achieved by duplicating or substituting, unless it is clear that competence is lacking in a particular area.

If, for example, a client has been dealing with an accounting firm for several years, then there should be little interest in changing that arrangement. Specific tax-shelter advice can be provided by an outsider without disturbing the fundamental relationships already in place.

Within the various disciplines, advisors will have different backgrounds and different specialties. It is widely acknowledged that we are in an era of specialization, and this can sometimes make the "general practitioner" uneasy and fearful of losing a client.

A key step in the planning process is for the advisors to meet occasionally without the client present. This provides an opportunity to exchange ideas, to discuss areas of specialty and to agree on an overall strategy for a specific client. It also provides an ideal opportunity to establish an agreement on who is going to do what and when. A possible drawback of this approach is that, where advisors are paid on an hourly basis, some clients are not enamoured with the prospect of receiving bills for advisors talking to each other, so sometimes this needs to be addressed in advance.

Without this step, it is common to find that advisors may duplicate each other's efforts or that there is really no effective communication among advisors, simply because of the fact that if the client is always present, certain topics of discussion are not feasible.

Who's in Charge Here?

The team approach referred to throughout this publication is, without a doubt, the best way to achieve value and performance for the client.

Unfortunately, teams need captains, and the typical team of advisors includes more than one captain. It is essential that the advisors agree on who is going to assume primary responsibility for seeing that the process is always moving toward a timely conclusion, arranging meetings and following up on requests for information.

For the team not to have a leader is not a good option. The client runs the risk of being confused and overwhelmed by being contacted several times on the same or similar issues. In addition, team members may have trouble avoiding an occasional element of competition.

Usually, this team leader (the real team leader in this example) is not the advisor with the greatest technical knowledge, nor the longest-serving, but the advisor with the closest relationship to the client. Who would the client call with a question or a problem, even if it were not necessarily in that advisor's specific area of expertise?

The team leader has to be recognized as such by other advisors on the team, and this is perhaps easier as the discussion focuses on relationship rather than expertise or seniority.

Succession Planning for the Financial Advisor's Practice

In Canada today, it is often estimated that as many as 50% of financial advisors have no succession plan in place. Indeed, it is even suggested that about 35% do not have a formal business plan. Perhaps these two statistics point to the same thing — financial advisors tend to view their own practice as an extension of themselves, rather than as a real business with all the advantages and disadvantages that being a real business entails.

When those of us who have been in the financial field for many years look back to when we first started, we can recall (just about) how we identified a viable prospective client — he or she was able to fog a mirror. We would talk to anyone who was willing to listen, and to many who were not. It would never occur to us to develop a business plan, nor to proactively define what an ideal client would look like. The number one priority was always survival.

At some point, though, a successful financial advisor begins to build a business, and begins to build an image and a reputation in the community as a valued advisor, rather than simply a seller of a product. When that happens, the relationship with the client changes, and the advisor assumes a sort of responsibility to see that the client is taken care of. If an advisor does a good job for a client, then he/she assumes an even greater responsibility — if, for example, a competitor approaches one of your clients with a new idea, the client's answer is often something along the lines of "I'm already taken care of, thank you. My advisor, John Smith, always keeps me up to date." Now, you are the shield that your client uses to keep other advisors away. You have to deliver the goods, so to speak, because if you don't, no one else will.

That shield, though, also defends your client from financial ruin. So, what happens to that shield in the event of your death or disability? Does it just break, leaving the client to look for another one? Or is there a backup system, a contingency plan?

We are, of course, familiar with the business succession process from our dealings with clients. In such a scenario, we might typically ask:

- In the event of your death, who would run the business?
- Who would own the business?
- Would it survive? Thrive?
- If you were unable to work because of a disability, who would take over?
- Where would your own income come from?

- How about if you suffered a critical illness?

- What will happen when you just don't want to work any more?

- How about when you want to work less? A lot less?

We know that our clients find these questions very difficult to answer. We do, too. Maybe if we wait long enough, we think, we'll get some inspiration from somewhere. Meanwhile, just like our clients, we tend to do nothing.

The average age of established financial advisors in Canada is about 50. As a group, financial advisors are disproportionately older than professionals in other fields, and the industry will see more turnover in the next 10 to 20 years than any other, although it is not yet clear what form this turnover will take. In some cases, unfortunately, it may take the form of simple abandonment, leaving others to sort out the mess and try to salvage some level of service for the clients.

A major complication comes from a profound recognition that the basic value component of a financial advisor's practice is the relationship with each client, not necessarily the size of the client's account. If a client chooses to do business with you because of you, then what does that say about your ability to sell that "file" to someone else? It does not mean that it cannot be done, but it does mean that the transfer process needs to be fundamentally different than might be the case in any other type of business. It means that, in order to satisfy that client on an ongoing basis, a successor in your practice has to provide continuity not just in technical and product expertise, but also to a considerable extent in temperament, and even in personality. This leads to a natural preference for internal succession, but internal succession will not necessarily make the process itself easier.

The very "hands on" nature of a financial advisory practice makes it extremely difficult to let go, and it often happens that the succession process is to a great extent ignored until it becomes a matter of urgency, by which time the opportunities for planning have, in large part, disappeared.

"If what you do is who you are, then when you don't, you're not." (Anonymous)

This is a common belief. Financial advisors identify so closely with what they do for a living that the entire succession question is quite traumatic. If we can make it into a process, perhaps some of the trauma will go away, but the issues are so significant and so varied that it will always be a challenge.

The optimal strategy is to assemble and digest as much information as possible, not just from outside sources but also from within our own practice. We assume that we know our own businesses and our own clients, but perhaps we don't know them as well as we think we do.

But let's start closer to home. Let's start by knowing ourselves.

One of the most interesting starting points is motivation: Why do you get up and go to work in the morning? Is it for money? Building a business? Fulfilling a commitment to clients? Habit? For the social aspect? The thrill of the hunt? The answer to this question will ultimately tell us a lot about what kind of succession planning process might be appropriate. But initially, it will drive the business plan, a plan that basically asks simple, but key, questions:

- Where is your practice today?

- Where would you like it to be in 5 years? 10 years?

- How will it get there?

- Do you have the available resources?

- What, if anything, do you need to do differently?

With a business plan in place, the next issue to consider is a contingency plan:

- What happens in the event of your disability?

- What happens in the event of your death?

- Are the proper resources in place?

- If not, what do you need to do?

The succession plan will be a natural extension of the business and contingency plans, and generally cannot be designed until they are completed. The succession plan is not an "if", but rather a "when", and therefore tends to be approached differently.

Just as our clients' ideas of retirement have changed over the years, so have ours. The rocking chair on the front porch isn't the ideal image any more, if it ever was, and each of us is looking for something different. A good starting point is to ask yourself a simple-sounding question — *"What do I want from retirement?"* This is a difficult question to answer, however, and goes a long way toward explaining why succession planning tends to be postponed or neglected in so many instances.

This simple question leads to an examination of a wide range of issues, among the major of which are:

- What kind of impact will my retirement have on the rest of my family? Is that impact acceptable to me?

- What kind of impact will it have on my friends, on my social activities? Will I lose the friends I have at work?

- Will I miss all the seminars and conferences I normally go to? How will I keep in touch with everyone? Do I want to keep in touch with everyone?

- What about the clients who are now my close friends? Can I tolerate seeing them handed over to someone else? Do I want to keep certain clients for myself?

- Financial advising may not be the most difficult work in the world, but it is mentally stimulating, even exhilarating at times — can I walk away from that? Will I be satisfied if I devote my problem-solving skills to just the daily crossword?

- What will I do instead? It's all well and good to think about what I'm retiring from, but what am I retiring to?

- Most of what I see refers to whether or not I can afford to retire, but the bigger issue is really whether I want to retire. Do I?

- Are there things that I gave up along the way to building a successful business that I would want to go back to when I have the time? Or was I a different person then? Have I really become what I do?

- Did I build a business? Or did I build a job? As mentioned earlier, if clients deal with me because of me, then am I really unable to retire anyway?

On this last point, the question of building a business or building a job, it is recommended that you take a look at *The E-myth Revisited,*[1] and at some of the discussion at www.e-myth.com.

The more the concept of retirement and succession planning comes to the fore, the more it seems that the era of the sole practitioner is coming to an end, although there are still many financial advisors for whom the independence of the sole practitioner is worth more than the advantages of a shared practice.

Once the decision to sell all or part of a practice, to retire or to semi-retire is made, the generally available options as to a suitable buyer can be reduced to:

---

[1] Michael E. Gerber, *The E-myth Revisited* (U.S.A.: HarperCollins, 1995).

- A family member;

- A colleague;

- An employee; or

- An outsider, whether an individual or a firm.

Regardless of which buyer seems appropriate, the first step in the process is to discuss the "big picture" with all stakeholders on a confidential basis — this will include family members, staff, colleagues, other professional advisors and perhaps even some trusted clients. Whatever the ultimate decision, you need the support of each of these stakeholders.

An important second step is to review the contract you have with each carrier with whom you do business. These contracts are legal documents and spell out your rights and obligations when it comes to transferring business to another advisor or group of advisors. The ability to transfer business varies by company and even by product line, so this is an important step — last-minute surprises can easily send a deal into a tailspin.

What Is It that You Have to Sell?

We all know that maintaining accurate records is important for many reasons, but how complete are the records? Can you look into your client database and identify the following, in addition to the usual factual identification issues?

- Revenue history of each client;

- Average revenue per client;

- Average revenue per client in each age group:

  - Under 35;

  - 35-50;

  - 51-65;

  - over 65.

- Longevity of each client;

- Source of each client;

- Type of product(s) for each client;

- Next scheduled client contact:

  - Renewal of term insurance;

- Renewal of GIC or other investment;

- Regular review.

- Frequency of contact:

  - By phone;

  - In person;

  - By e-mail;

  - By mail.

- Employer;

- Type of industry;

- Employment income;

- Other earned income;

- Unearned income;

- Net worth;

- Eligibility for Small Business Gains Exemption;

- Small Business Gains Exemption crystallization;

- Capital gains tax liability in estate;

- Property outside home province;

- Property outside Canada;

- Citizenship(s);

- Heirs outside Canada;

- Details of will (date, major provisions and beneficiaries, etc.);

- Family trust in place; and

- Anticipated inheritances.

Which of these items of information would be of interest to you, or to a potential buyer? Unlike with buying a car, there is no opportunity for a test drive other than a "snapshot" of the client base, and there is no real "upside" for the buyer if this cannot be demonstrated.

Have clients always dealt with you personally, as opposed to staff members? If so, how would they feel about a transition?

Here, there is a difference between financial buyers, who are simply looking to expand their existing business, and strategic buyers, who are looking to increase their presence in a specific market. Generally speaking, a strategic buyer tends to pay a higher price, but of course this depends on your ability to demonstrate the strategic worth of your database. This will in turn have an impact on value, hence on purchase price — for example, an aging client base might be a negative for a buyer looking for a quick return on his investment but a positive opportunity for a buyer who specializes in estate planning.

A key point to make here is that there is no such thing as an objective, totally realistic and definite "value" of a practice. The value will depend largely on who is looking at the practice. From a potential buyer's point of view, he or she will be looking very carefully at all of the component parts to make sure that the necessary value is there. It will not be sufficient simply to look at the client inventory.

Similarly, it will not be enough from your point of view to simply look at the potential buyer's ability to pay what you consider to be a fair price for the business. Before even entertaining any offer, part of the seller's thought process has to include:

- What does an ideal purchaser look like to you?

- What does an ideal purchaser look like from your support staff's point of view?

- What does an ideal purchaser look like from your clients' point of view?

These may be three very different images, or they may be quite similar, but the questions demonstrate the importance of obtaining input from the various stakeholders. Obviously, if a particular buyer were to complete the purchase only to find that all of the staff are leaving or all of the clients are leaving, you would have a very unhappy buyer.

Each type of buyer has advantages and disadvantages, and these will be factors in the decision regarding whom to sell to.

Sale to a Family Member

Advantages:

- continuity for clients;

- firm can retain identity;

- positive image of longevity;
- previous leader can remain involved if appropriate;
- a gentle transition;
- a gradual transition;
- typically greater financial flexibility.

Disadvantages:

- potential problems with "fair vs. equal" debate;
- seller requires mentoring skills as well as management skills;
- lack of objectivity with performance criteria;
- difficulty for seller to "let go";
- ongoing involvement of parent not always wanted;
- tendency to overestimate children's ability;
- emotional rather than logical decision?

Sale to a Colleague

Advantages:

- easy transition for clients;
- degree of "fit" already determined;
- more objective approach to financing;
- gradual transition possible;
- experience.

Disadvantages:

- long lead time required;
- may change character of firm;
- less ongoing input from seller?

Sale to an Employee

Advantages:

- buyer knows the clients;

- gradual transition;
- preserve character of firm.

Disadvantages:

- different skill set required;
- may need lots of mentoring;
- long lead time required.

Sale to an Outsider

Advantages:

- easiest option for seller;
- financially "arm's length".

Disadvantages:

- may be difficult for clients;
- may be difficult for support staff;
- sudden transition may be disruptive;
- unusual to find a fully qualified buyer.

It is evident that no single choice has all of the advantages, and none is without its disadvantages, so, as with most issues, it becomes a series of preferences and compromises. There are, however, factors you can identify and document (preferably well in advance) to enhance the probability of concluding a sale of your practice on a solid and profitable basis. Factors such as the following will go a long way toward demonstrating value to a potential purchaser:

- What kind of reputation does your firm have in the industry? Involvement in professional associations, rather than just member-ship, can enhance status and therefore value.

- What kind of reputation does your firm have in the community? Involvement in charity events, fund raising, good citizenship can all contribute to status and value — even though they have no direct relationship to business, they definitely factor into the goodwill com-putation.

- How much of your new business comes as a result of referrals from existing clients? Is this documented?

- What kind of referral systems do you have in place? Are they well documented?

- Aside from active referrals, what kind of working relationship do you have with accountants in your area? Are there key contacts you rely on? Do you refer business to them? Is this well documented?

- What about lawyers in your area?

- Have you participated in any study groups with other advisors?

- Is your client management system as up to date as it should be?

- What kind of networking do you normally do? Is it formalized at all? Are there regular networking functions you attend? Are the main contacts documented? Could someone else step into your shoes there?

- What are the skill levels of your staff? Do any of them have unique skills? What kind of industry qualifications do they have? Do they regularly attend educational sessions and courses? Are any of them licensed?

- Is staff turnover low?

- Does your practice have a spotless compliance record?

- Is your particular market niche highly competitive, or does your practice enjoy a leadership position? Is this documented?

- If a potential purchaser were to "Google" your name or your firm's name, what would they find? Does the image presented match with what you think it should be? If you have a website, does it convey a professional image? Do you have any idea of how many "hits" it regularly receives?

- Do you produce and/or distribute a client newsletter? Where does the information come from? Is it something you create yourself? Do you personalize a third-party subscription? Do you do any kind of regular follow-up with newsletter recipients? Is feedback documented?

- What kind of client appreciation events do you normally have on a regular basis? Is client feedback from these events documented?

Put yourself in the buyer's position for a moment — if you were to see full documentation of all the above issues in a particular practice, how likely is it that your opinion of the practice, and hence of its value, would be enhanced? There is nothing unique in the above list, and many practitioners routinely do all of these things — what makes the difference is having all of them documented so that someone who wasn't there at the time they ocurred can see the impact and appreciate the overall "flavour" of the practice. This helps to ensure optimal "fit" and tends to make the sale easier, or at least makes the decision process more reliable. A good rule of thumb is always — document, document, document.

Once you identify a logical successor/purchaser, then, if the purchase is unlikely to take place right away, or if there is a lengthy transition period, it is advisable to enter into a buy-sell agreement. The degree of formality in the agreement may depend on the relationship between the parties, but it is nonetheless important that an agreement be entered into. As with agreements in a client's business, a buy-sell agreement in this instance becomes a minimum standard, a "safety net," just in case things go awry.

Buy-Sell Agreement Provisions

Typically, an agreement between financial advisors in a succession environment will include items such as:

- In the event of the death of the future vendor, the survivor agrees to purchase the practice using the agreed upon valuation approach or formula.

- The purchase price will be paid in cash (if using life insurance funding) or over a period of time (if using strictly an "earn out" approach).

- The future vendor agrees to sell the practice on reaching a specific age, or on a specific date, again using an agreed-to valuation approach or formula.

- The future vendor also agrees to sell in the event of a total and permanent disability.

- A commitment that both parties will devote their efforts to the practice itself, and will not develop business on their own account. This would include some concept of "full time" efforts, although this is often difficult to determine.

- Circumstances under which the agreement may be cancelled without penalty on either side.

- How to "undo" the deal if the sharing of clients has already begun at the time of a disagreement.

Discussions of insurance funding would be the same as for clients, although hopefully with a different level of appreciation for the process. As usual, valuation is subjective rather than objective, and may well be different in different circumstances. For example, a value agreed on for a buyout at retirement would assume some kind of transition period on the part of the vendor, but of course a buyout on death or disability would have no such transition and might therefore have a lower value.

Preparing to Sell

The decision to sell all or part of your practice is neither one that is taken lightly, nor one that can be implemented in a hurry. Between the time of the decision and the actual sale, there are a few things that can be done to maximize the success of the transaction, not simply from a financial point of view but also from a procedural point of view.

We outlined above the points to document for a potential purchaser, and this period is an ideal time to review those issues. While doing so, it is also an ideal time to look at your practice through the eyes of a purchaser rather than a vendor. Do you have a part of your client base that does not "fit" with the rest, a part that could be sold off separately to allow you to focus all your efforts on the core group of clients?

In addition, this is a good time to make a complete inventory of what makes up your practice — clients, technology, staff, goodwill and so on. It is important to look at these issues as objectively as possible before getting to the issue of valuation.

Valuation

This is where the crux of the matter lies. The issue of valuation is part of the litmus test of the business you have built over the years. If the value is not what you hoped it to be, the sale will be a much less enthusiastic process.

As a part of this vital component, take a few sheets of paper and write down your thoughts with regard to the following:

- Why do you want to sell?

- When do you want to sell?

- Over what period of time?

- Is this a part of a long-term plan or a sudden change of heart?

- Do you know what your clients will think?

- Do you know what your staff will think?

- Realistically, what do you think the business is worth?

- What does the ideal purchaser look like?

- What does the "wrong" purchaser look like?

- If you were unable to find the right buyer, is there an acceptable Plan B?

Armed with this information, you can then begin to look at value. It may be advisable to pay for a professional valuation, and the typical cost of $10,000 to $20,000 is often a worthwhile investment, representing a small percentage of the value of the business being valued. However, there have been examples of a valuation being dramatically at odds with the owner's perception of value, but where the owner's idea of value was eventually supported, so it is important to have your own idea of value even before the process begins. You know your practice better than anyone else does, especially when you go through this reflective process in advance.

One obvious advantage of a valuation done well in advance is that it might reveal shortcomings in the practice that can be rectified before the sale process begins.

In the June 2004 issue of *Investment Advisor* magazine, Mark Tibergien, the pre-eminent authority on practice valuation and a partner with Moss Adams LLP, wrote the following:

> For most people in the advisory business, the question of practice value arises in purchase and sale situations. The owner often has an inflated perception of the value of his or her firm, and the prospective buyer is usually certain he's overpaying. There are instances, however, in which those roles are reversed. For example, in the context of a divorce, shareholder breakup, or other litigation, typically the owner will say, "This business is entirely dependent on me. Without me, all the clients would go away."

Clearly, value can be a subjective issue. To maximize practice value, you have to believe that you are entirely dispensable, which of course goes against what most of us have believed all along.

When a buyer looks at a practice, he or she is looking for future profits, not current profits, and this boils down to the client database, its transferability and its "fit" with the business style of the buyer. My favourite sales trainer, Jeffrey Gitomer, has asked a great question we should all keep in mind: "What are the things that you say you do for your clients that your competitors don't say they do for their clients?"[2] We don't have any unique edge in what we say we do, and the value we bring has to be in actual performance, things we do that make clients stay with us and refer their friends to us.

Mark Tibergien also asks the following questions, all of which are indicators of value:

- What is the unique value proposition that attracts clients to your firm and keeps them there?

- Have your net client revenues grown at a rate greater than market growth and inflation over the last five years?

- Do you have specialties or industry niches that represent a significant portion of your business?

- Are your client relationships institutionalized or specific-person-centric?

- How many people [in your firm] are currently legitimate potential successors?

- Can you state with confidence that they are prepared for the transition?

- If something happens to you, what will happen to your clients?

In addition, says Tibergien, "Most advisors have an inflated perception of value. They think it's tied to the number of years they've spent in the business but value is a function of the future".

So what is the value? There are a few different methods of determining value; people typically use more than one, and then work with a range of values. There are numerous resources to help with the valuation question, some of the more prominent being:

www.FPTransitions.com

This is a U.S. website discussing the sale and purchase of a financial advisory practice.

---

[2] As heard, for example, in Gitomer's presentation on the DVD, *The Jim Rohn 2001 Weekend Event.*

www.fpanet.org

This is the official website of the American Financial Planning Association, with many useful articles. They also publish *Succession Planning Strategies for the Financial Planner: A Complete Resource Guide*, by David K. Goad (2nd ed., 2005).

A great deal has been written on the details of valuation principles, citing multiples, cash flows, revenue stream discounts and assets under management. Generally speaking, there is little consensus on what constitutes the right deal in any given situation, and we have to conclude that the ultimate answer is whatever gets the buyer and the seller to put pen to paper. More often than not, the optimal deal occurs when each of the parties feels that the other got the better of the deal.

Typical averages would include:

- a multiple of gross revenues, somewhere in the range of 1 to 1.5 times the gross commission income. If a significant portion of the revenue is fee-based rather than commission-based, the multiple may be higher, in the range of 2 times revenue. The main issue here is whether it is realistic to base value on gross revenues as opposed to net cash flow. Does it imply that a new owner would have the same cost structure or the same level of efficiency as the original owner? It is advisable to look at the net revenue as well as the gross, to make sure that the assumptions are reasonable. If one advisor spares no expense in the quest for new clients and another is more frugal, then the value of the two practices might be significantly different, even though a simple multiple of gross might indicate otherwise. Rules of thumb are not always reliable, they just happen to be convenient — it is possible to get too attached to them, and a common sense approach always has to be applied.

- As a rule, multiples are applied to a 3-year average.

- Renewal commissions and trailer fees are often treated differently, using a multiple of anywhere from 1 to 3 times earnings.

- Similarly, assets under management may be valued at between 0.5% and 2%, depending on the type, duration and active management requirement.

The objective of determining value, apart from the obvious purchase price implications, is to try to assess how much value the practice as a going concern adds to the income that an advisor would earn by his own efforts without the book of business. As an example, if a practice generated gross revenues of $500,000, then the base calculation might be along the following lines:

Gross revenue	$500,000
Direct expenses	200,000 (tends to average 40%)
Overhead costs	200,000 (also 40%)
Profit	100,000 (pre-tax)

Direct expenses in this example include commissions paid to professional members of the firm, including owners. In other words, a commission-earning advisor would have earned $200,000 in any event, without having ownership of the practice. Ownership of the practice, in this example, provides an additional $100,000 of pre-tax earnings to the owner. How much should he/she pay to earn this extra $100,000?

If he/she were to invest $1,000,000 in a bank account paying, say, 6%, he/she would earn $60,000 pre-tax — with no appreciable risk. If he/she paid $1,000,000 to buy a practice that paid him an additional $100,000, then this would represent a rate of return of 10% on that invested capital. Is this a good investment? What kind of risk is there? There is more risk than in a bank account, but how much more? The risk is a risk to capital, not just to income, so it needs to be considered seriously. How does he/she mitigate the risk? (That is one of the functions of the buyer's due diligence in the decision making process.)

The question the buyer has to ask is, "If I pay myself a fair income in exchange for the work I do in the practice, is there any money left over?" If the answer is "no", the business that the owner has built over the years is not really providing any value (although that realization would be traumatic for the owner). If the answer is "yes", and if it is transferable to another owner, then the business itself has a value in addition to the revenue that a principal earns by his or her own efforts.

Current demographics suggest that in the near future there will be more sellers than buyers. One would expect prices to decline, but, while this may be the average result, a well-managed practice producing a healthy revenue stream on a consistent basis will still command a respectable price. At any rate, buyers will have the luxury of being more selective.

How Will the Purchase Price Be Paid?

In an ideal world, perhaps all purchases would be made in cash. As soon as you would agree on a price for your business, the buyer would write you a cheque and everyone would live happily ever after. In the real world, things are quite different. The financing options available typically vary according to the relationship between the buyer and the seller.

A sale to a family member usually offers the greatest flexibility, as there is the greatest degree of trust and the greatest desire for the transfer to be successful. As an example — Jim Green has a successful life insurance and financial planning practice. His children, Dave and Heather, have worked in the business for several years, and are now ready to take over and let Jim enjoy his semi-retirement. It would be counter-productive for Dave and Heather to borrow the $2,000,000 to buy out their father if they will ultimately inherit the business anyway. Jim has no great desire for capital to invest elsewhere, and is happy to receive a comfortable income in addition to income from his own investments.

Jim agrees to have the children pay him an income from the business of $100,000 a year, pre-tax. Eventually, the children will inherit the business and will be faced with a tax liability on capital gains, so they agree to take over ownership of a life insurance policy in the amount of $500,000, thus relieving Jim of the obligation to pay ongoing premiums.

Jim's wife, Jane, has never been involved in the business at any level, and is not part of the succession process. Jim has sufficient life insurance and the two of them have enough other assets for her income, in the event of his death, to be sufficient without any reliance on the business. If that were not the case, Jim could provide additional life insurance coverage so that Jane could receive independent capital on his death.

Meanwhile, Jim will continue to work in the business as and when he sees fit, spending time with special clients, bringing in new business and occasionally troubleshooting.

Is this fair market value? Perhaps not, although Dave and Heather will eventually pay capital gains tax on the fair market value. (It should be mentioned, however, that, depending on amounts and structure, it may be possible to do a freeze at today's value and let the growth accrue in the children's names.)

Is it fair? It is if Jim thinks it is. It would not be a viable solution in a non-family environment, of course. Even in this case, there are potential problems to be concerned about. What happens in the event that Jim becomes disabled and is unable to participate in the business at all? Will Dave and Heather be able to cope and continue to pay Jim? If not, what is the remedy? The three of them also need a buy-sell agreement or at least a business agreement outlining the rights and obligations of each of them and covering contingency issues such as death, disability and disagreement.

One of the major issues in a family succession is that we tend to focus on ownership at the expense of management. If Dave and Heather are competent in the areas of client relationships and problem solving, but have none of their father's management skills, then this should be recognized, probably by hiring a manager, even on a part-time basis.

Another potential issue revolves around the closeness of family relationships. If Dave and/or Heather prove to be poorly suited as successors to Jim, will they be fired? Or will they hang in there, simply because they are family, even at the expense of the business itself? It is important to agree on some kind of performance criteria, even for family members, and then those criteria can form part of any business agreement. Parents typically feel a sense of obligation to their children's success, and it is important to balance this sense of obligation with an occasional reality check along the way.

An internal succession, whether involving colleagues or employees, is an increasingly popular option. Properly structured, it will provide many of the benefits of a family succession:

- it allows for a gradual transition;

- it provides the owner with ongoing client contact; and

- it is a gentler method for clients.

One of the issues faced in this type of succession is that the owner may be unable to "let go" and may get in the way of the succession. This is perhaps understandable in a family situation, but will invariably lead to conflict in a non-family succession.

Nonetheless, this gentler succession does allow for some flexibility in payment method, typically allowing for

- buyout for cash or bank financing; or

- "earn out" over time.

Again, the cash buyout is unlikely and, in the right environment, unnecessary. An "earn out" allows for a staged transition that benefits the seller and the clients as well as the buyer. Instead of struggling to write a cheque for $2,000,000, the buyer agrees to pay the seller, say, interest on the declining balance at bank prime, plus an annual amount equal to 25% of the net income of the business, subject to an annual minimum of $100,000. There is no down payment in this example, and the risk is largely on the shoulders of the vendor, so there needs to be a significant degree of trust in this arrangement. Since the vendor is still actively involved, if he or she chooses to be, the risk is mitigated, but it still exists. The annual obligation for the purchaser should be high enough to be a "stretch", but not so high as to be a disincentive — it needs to be taken seriously, but it should not keep all the parties awake at night.

For an outside buyer, there is typically a lot less flexibility. The vendor wants the sale to take place, of course, but he is less interested in being bought out with his own money. The normal type of "earn out" used in family and internal succession is less appropriate here, as it tends to hand too much control to the buyer and gives the seller an unacceptable amount of risk. It is usual for a sale to an outside buyer to lead to a fairly sudden departure by the original owner, and he/she therefore has considerably less input into the ongoing business, thus less opportunity to make sure things are going according to plan.

If any kind of "earn out" is appropriate, it will usually be at a higher price, to reflect the increased risk, and will typically involve a significant down payment. For example, the purchaser may use $500,000 of bank financing, and then pay the balance on an "earn out" basis similar to the one outlined above. Again, a business agreement will outline the relative rights and obligations and will provide for various contingencies.

Regardless of the buyout method used, the role of life insurance and, where appropriate, disability insurance should not be underestimated. We emphasize this to our clients, and should include it in our own planning activities.

Summary

It is clear that succession planning for a financial advisory practice is not entirely dissimilar to that for our clients. The details differ, but the principles are exactly the same. We know that the ways to ensure optimal results for all of the stakeholders are to:

- Start the process well in advance. It should not be left to when we've decided to retire or slow down, but rather should be begun during the active building phase of our practice. The traditional image of the sole practitioner is changing rapidly and dramatically — the complexity of the business has lead to specialization and to groups of advisors working together, each advisor in his/her own specialty. Even without establishing a formal relationship, many advisors are developing strategic alliances as their careers advance. The entrepreneurial freedom of "going it alone" is no longer consistent with maximizing long-term results, and the choices available can go a long way toward providing real benefits to both advisors and clients.

- The first step is to be clear about what you want from the process: capital, income, total retirement, partial retirement or just the opportunity to slow down a little and play more golf or take more vacations.

- Communicate with stakeholders. keep family, employees, colleagues and clients informed about upcoming changes. Solicit their opinions and advice.

- Look at all of the available sale alternatives — to a family member, colleague, employee or outsider — and realistically assess the merits of each option.

- Don't try to do everything yourself. If you feel the need for a "succession coach," they are not hard to find. Rely on the advice of others who have successfully navigated the same waters. Obtain professional advice from your legal and accounting advisors. Talk to retired clients and ask them what, if anything, they would do differently if they were retiring today. We cannot possibly live long enough to make all of the mistakes ourselves, so we need to pay attention to the experience of others, especially of those we respect.

Stephen R. Covey is one of the great authors on leadership and mastery. In his *Seven Habits of Highly Effective People*[3] and the co-authored *First Things First*,[4] he effectively summarizes the time conflicts that we all face. Dr. Covey divides our time into four quadrants:

Quadrant 1	**Quadrant 2**
Urgent and important	Important, but not urgent
Quadrant 3	**Quadrant 4**
Urgent and not important	Not important and not urgent

If we look at this table and ask where we spend most of our time, most of us will agree that we spend the vast majority of our time in Quadrant 1, working on projects and tasks that are both urgent and important. Our daily "to do" list is filled with these items.

---

[3] Stephen R. Covey, *The Seven Habits of Highly Effective People: Restoring the Character Ethic* (U.S.A.: Simon and Schuster, 1989).

[4] Stephen R. Covey, A. Roger Merrill and Rebecca R. Merrill, *First Things First* (U.S.A.: Fireside, 1995).

After a while in the high-pressure environment of Quadrant 1 activities, we need a break, so we flee to Quadrant 3 or Quadrant 4. There, we can play golf, read a novel or magazine, watch television or go to a movie. Fully recharged, we can then go back to Quadrant 1 and refocus on business priorities.

Quadrant 2, working on items that are important but not urgent, sees little if any of our activity. And yet that is where our really important work is done. Succession Planning is a Quadrant 2 activity. It is important, vitally important, but it is not urgent. For some of us, if we wait long enough, succession planning will become urgent as well as important — it will move over into Quadrant 1 — but by then we will have missed out on a lot of the planning opportunities, as there will simply not be enough time to give the process the preparation and recognition that it deserves.

As Michael Gerber says in *The E-myth Revisited*, we need to spend more time working on our business, rather than just working in our business.

CHAPTER 16

The Business Owner's Perspective

J ohn C. Maxwell, an American guru in the field of leadership excellence, has written that "A legacy is created only when a person puts his organization into the position to do great things without him".[1]

There is little doubt that succession planning is one of the most important exercises for any business owner. If the business ceases to exist the moment its founder is no longer on the scene, the contribution of the business owner to society is significantly minimized. An equivalent in the sporting world would be to carry the football all the way to the one-yard line, only to then fall and drop the ball. No one will remember the brilliance of the run, just the fact that it ended in failure.

It is strange, then, that many business owners neglect or simply postpone the succession planning process. In February 2005, CIBC World Markets published a report entitled *Are Canadian entrepreneurs ready for retirement?*[2] The report, compiled by Benjamin Tal, shows how serious this crisis is becoming. Among the report's findings are the following points:

1. When asked for their projected retirement dates,

    a. 22% suggested it would be before 2010;

    b. 29% suggested it would be between 2010 and 2019;

    c. 24% suggested it would be between 2020 and 2029; and

    d. 25% said it would be later than 2029.

This means that *1.2 trillion dollars in business assets is poised to change hands between now and 2010.* Intergenerational turnover on this scale is unprecedented. Accordingly, the cost of faulty planning will also be astronomical — measured in terms of additional taxes payable because of inefficient structures for succession, reduced productivity in organizations that barely survive the process, related job losses, "fire sale" prices and increased rates of bankruptcy.

---

[1] John C. Maxwell, *The 21 Irrefutable Laws of Leadership: Follow Them and People Will Follow You* (Nashville: Thomas Nelson, 1998), 219.

[2] CIBC World Markets Report, *Are Canadian Entrepreneurs Ready For Retirement?* (CIBC World Markets, 2005).

2. In spite of the immediacy of the problem and the importance of the issue itself, only two in five small business owners have a clear plan for exiting their business.

3. As many as 60% of entrepreneurs between the ages of 55 and 64 *have not yet started* to discuss their exit plans with family or business partners.

4. In this same group of 55- to 64-year-olds, only about 15% have definite plans to transfer or sell the business to a family member. About 17% are not sure — they may transfer to family members but have not yet decided. The balance, over 67%, have decided not to transfer to a family member.

5. Between 2001 and 2004, the number of self-employed people over the age of 65 who are still working increased by 33%. This is not necessarily a good thing or a bad thing; it depends on the reasons. If someone normally considered to be beyond normal retirement age is still working because he or she wants to continue working (and this is becoming more common), this development is a good thing. If continuing to work is driven simply by economic necessity or if it is because the business owner has never been able to find a suitable alternative, then it would be a bad thing.

It is evident throughout this report that the topic of succession planning is simply not being addressed with sufficient urgency. *In the next 13 years, more than 50% of Canadian entrepreneurs are planning to retire, and the majority of them have not yet considered how this is going to happen.*

Nowhere in the report is it suggested that entrepreneurs cannot afford to retire. Money is not the issue. Advance planning and preparation are the issues. Is it possible that business owners believe that, when the time comes, they will simply hang a "For Sale" sign on the door and wait for the offers to come flooding in? Or that, if they wait long enough, other entrepreneurs will approach them and offer to buy the business?

Or is it more likely that most business owners don't really know what is involved in the succession planning process, how to get it started, nor even whom to approach to discuss the topic?

In this chapter, we will look at the issues from the business owner's point of view rather than from the advisor's point of view. We will look at some of the "big picture" issues, then discuss some of the most common questions asked by business owners. The objective is to help business owners feel more comfortable with the process.

The Basics of Succession Planning

When an individual starts a business, as a sole proprietor, as a partner in a partnership or as a shareholder in a corporation (often the sole share-holder), he/she commits to the business everything he/she has, typically in terms of money as well as time and energy. The business enterprise tends to become all-consuming. The initial stages are often the time when the major objective is survival. Trying to keep the business vibrant and growing while maintaining some semblance of a normal life is often impossible, and things always seem to involve one compromise after another.

The typical conflict of withdrawing enough money to live on and at the same time leaving enough money in the business to provide for expansion opportunities is just one example of the challenges a new business faces. At this early stage, there is little thought of succession planning, as there are just too many more important things to be concerned with. To look after other family members, it is normally sufficient to buy some life insurance, along with some disability insurance to provide income in the event of a serious illness or accident.

As time passes, the business looks like it will prosper. Business is good, income is good, and the future looks bright. This is a time to make hay while the sun shines, to take advantage of the conditions and grow the business as much as possible. It is unlikely, however, to be a time for succession planning. It will be left until later.

As usually happens, "later" is not a time, but rather an attitude. There are always more urgent, more entertaining things to do. Succession planning never makes it to the top of the list. Unless there is a problem event, such as death, a critical illness, a serious accident or a permanent disability: then it becomes a priority. But by then it is often too late, and many of the options that are usually part of the planning process are no longer available.

The advantages of addressing the process of succession planning, of thinking about the issues and implementing solutions where appropriate, include:

- A greater chance that the business will survive;

- Improved family harmony;

- Cash for surviving family members;

- Uninterrupted service for clients;

- Minimization of taxes;

- Ongoing opportunities for employees;

- Enhanced employee loyalty;

- Retirement income for owners;

- Peace of mind;

- Predictable voting control;

- Greater flexibility and choices.

Note that minimizing taxes is just one component. We sometimes see plans that are built only on paying as little tax as possible, but they rarely reflect the true wishes of the business owner. It is vitally important for the business owner to decide what the key issues are for him/her and the family, and then build a plan around those issues.

Succession Planning typically involves just a few central concerns:

1. In the event of the death of the business owner, who takes over?

2. In the event of a permanent disability or serious accident or illness, who takes over?

3. When the owner wants to retire, who steps into his/her shoes?

4. In each of the above instances, where will income come from?

5. Who will pay taxes, and with what?

Of course, many plans are quite complex in nature, but they all start from the same basic concerns.

Who Should I Talk to In Order To Get the Planning Started?

Most business owners have several advisors on whom they rely, and there will be a natural tendency to begin with one of them. While each advisor will eventually have a vital role to play, it is important to begin with the right one. The list of advisors will include:

- A lawyer;

- An accountant;

- A banker;

- A business partner;

- A financial advisor;

- A spiritual advisor;

- A spouse;

- Children; and/or

- A close friend.

As is often the case, there is no right answer for all situations — the lawyer might be the right choice in one situation, the accountant in another, the spiritual advisor in another, or sometimes just a close friend whose opinion you respect. It may seem surprising to include a spiritual advisor on the list, but it is indicative of the fact that the key issues are emotional and family oriented rather than financial or technical in nature. In fact, generally speaking, **the difference between a succession plan that succeeds and one that fails has little to do with finances, taxes or corporate structure.** In essence, the plan that succeeds does so because it addresses the special personal, emotional and family priorities of the business owner, as well as the needs of the business itself, any business partners and the employees of the business.

So how should you decide where to start? One simple test is often all that is required. Many advisors, if not most advisors, are conditioned by their training and experience to answer questions that you ask. But in most cases, the answers are not difficult at all. The hard part is in figuring out what the questions should be. So you need to start the process with someone who can help you identify the questions, someone who doesn't get hung up on solutions and doesn't get carried away by the technical issues involved. If a particular advisor is someone you talk to just to get an answer to a tax question, for example, perhaps that advisor is not the one you should start with.

The succession planning process is very much a "big picture" exercise and is holistic in nature. The advisor who helps you get the process started should be someone who is comfortable with this approach. As the details become clearer, other advisors have different roles to play.

What Kinds of Things Should We Talk About to Begin with?

Is the succession plan a means for you to:

- Retire completely?

- Walk away and never look back, as if the business never existed?

- Retire to a tropical island somewhere?

- Work fewer hours?

- Become a better golfer?

- Spend more time with your spouse?

- Step back from a business in which technology ceased to make sense years ago?

- Work only with favourite clients?

- Be the "rainmaker"?

- Take more vacations?

- Bring one or more of your children into the business right away?

- Make sure your spouse is not dependent on the business for future income if he/she has no desire to be?

- Make sure your children inherit a healthy, vibrant business?

- Make sure your family is financially secure?

- Make sure key employees become owners?

- Make sure your employees continue to look after your clients?

- Provide you with capital to invest elsewhere?

- Provide you with capital or income for philanthropic purposes?

- Provide you with ongoing income for life?

Obviously, the answer to this question will, to a considerable extent, determine the type of planning strategies to be used. As the old saying goes, "If you don't know where you're going, any road will get you there", and this is true in succession planning, too. Unclear objectives and motivations lead to plans that are not really yours, but rather represent an amalgam of many other plans for many other people.

You don't want a plan that's tailor-made for people like you, you want a plan that's tailor-made for you, and there can be a significant difference.

This will involve other people's dreams, fears, objectives and priorities, not just those of the business owner. All of the people involved, whether they be family members, co-workers, shareholders, key managers or trusted advisors, will in many cases be thinking about issues they have never thought about before, in a context that may be completely alien to them. After all, how many times does a typical business owner arrange to transfer ownership of the business?

Initially, it is important to remember that, with very few exceptions, decisions made tentatively today need not be irreversible tomorrow.

It is therefore advisable to consider two very valuable components:

1. A safety net, just in case everything falls apart; and

2. An escape hatch, just in case you change your mind.

If a plan you consider contains both of these elements, then the process itself becomes a lot less threatening. We will consider a couple of these strategies in some detail a little later.

This first step is crucial, and should not be rushed. Discuss your thoughts with other family members, with other shareholders, with key employees. Make sure to consider all of the alternatives. Sometimes, this first step can take months, which can be difficult for an entrepreneur who habitually makes decisions in the blink of an eye. It is probably, however, the greatest single determinant of success, since it usually leads to a plan to which all the parties are committed.

Private Company Ownership

In the vast majority of succession planning ventures, we are dealing with an ownership interest in a private company. Such an interest is not a liquid asset, although it may itself own one or more liquid assets. As a going concern, it will not normally attract a host of buyers with large bank balances.

In a family business environment, we have the added complication of family members. Would a non-family member fit in as a shareholder? Would that create conflict within the family? What about a family member's spouse? What kind of havoc would divorce create within the succession plan?

In a private company environment, there are special problems that tend to not exist in other types of businesses.

As an example, does an entrepreneur create a business or a job? This question, posed by Michael Gerber in his excellent book "The E-myth", is central to the planning process. If you create a job, then you really have nothing to sell, or not much to sell, anyway. Suppose you build and sell the world's greatest widgets, each one of which is crafted by hand by you personally; if you were to decide to retire, what would you have to sell? Customer lists, perhaps, but not much else, unless you were to bring in an apprentice and teach him/her how to do your job in the same way.

So there's a danger in trying to build the business on the foundation of your own individual talents alone. And yet that's really what drives people to become entrepreneurs in the first place — they don't fit in anywhere as employees, or they have a vision of something to create that cannot be created within an existing employment framework. To put it less diplomatically, most entrepreneurs are control freaks. This quality, which enables them to succeed as business owners, often prevents them from building a business that maximizes the ability to be transferred, whether by sale or gift, to employees, children or outsiders.

Generally, the success rate of intergenerational transfers is about 30%. So if we start with ten businesses, three would make it to the next generation and just one to the third generation. Perhaps the entrepreneurial mindset is responsible for much of this. It is extremely difficult for an entrepreneur to step back from the business he/she has built and prepare to release the reins. An excellent book devoted to this topic is *Letting Go: Preparing Yourself to Relinquish Control of the Family Business.*[3]

Fair Versus Equal

One of the more crucial parts of the succession debate within a family business revolves around the children of the business owner or owners. Do you want to treat the children equally, or should they be treated fairly? (Yes, there usually is a difference.)

This is best illustrated by means of an example. Suppose Bill and Joan are the owners of Jobi Enterprises Ltd., a family engineering business with a value of around $6,000,000. They have three children, all in their 30's:

> Michael is an engineer at Jobi, and is married to Nicole. Ellen is a lawyer, and is married to Edgar, who is also a lawyer. Richard is a stockbroker, who was recently divorced from Penny.

When Bill and Joan sat down to discuss the idea of succession planning, the first obstacle they encountered was the fair/equal debate. Joan's first reaction was that they should arrange to leave the business to the children equally, but would that be the right thing to do? She acknowledged

---

[3] Craig E. Aronoff, *Letting Go: Preparing Yourself to Relinquish Control of the Family Business* (Marietta, Georgia: Family Enterprise Publishers, 2003).

that Michael would be running the business, but surely the children would be able to work things out?

There are not too many alternatives to consider:

• leave everything equally to the three children;

• leave the business to Michael, and everything else to the other two; or

• try to equalize without splitting up ownership of the business.

The first option, leaving everything to the children equally, is unlikely to succeed. Michael, working in the business, would have to take into account the preferences of his brother and sister in every significant decision in every area of the business. As the business driver, he might decide to re-invest profits in the business, to produce even greater future profits or to branch out into different areas of specialty. His brother and sister might be expected to have different views — they might want large cash dividends instead of the re-investment Michael favours. It looks like equality and suggests fairness, but it results in neither.

The second option, leaving the business to Michael, and dividing the rest of the assets between the other two, is a much better result for the business. It allows Michael to run the business as he sees fit, based on his past experience and expertise. However, it denies Ellen and Richard even the appearance of equality.

The third, leaving the business to Michael and trying to equalize via other assets, can be a useful solution, but is not without its own difficult issues. Perhaps, for this to work out perfectly from an equality point of view, the estate would need to total $18,000,000, so that each child could receive $6,000,000. It is unusual for an estate to consist of so many non-business assets, although it could be done (often by providing for the purchase of life insurance to make up the shortfall). But then what about taxes? Transferring a $6,000,000 business asset might involve as much as $1,200,000 of tax on capital gains — who would pay that, and where would the money come from? In addition, this approach to equality would in all likelihood not be fair — if you were one of the three children, would you rather receive a $6,000,000 business or $6,000,000 in cash? Clearly, those two items are not equal in value, even though they are equal in dollar amount.

There is really no right or wrong approach to this question — the point is that it must be addressed and, ideally, communicated to and discussed with other stakeholders in the process. Sometimes, it seems as if it would be much easier if there were a definitive "right" answer for every situation, but that just isn't the case. In all honesty, it can be hard work, but then most business owners are used to hard work.

With the above comments as background information, we will now look at some of the more typical questions that arise during the succession planning process. While a particular question may not apply to your specific situation, it may still be helpful to review all of them, as there are no "airtight compartments" here, and one area of concern tends to spill over into several others — the questions themselves are intended to be an area of focus for the ensuing discussion.

I Can't Decide Which of My Children Might Best Be Able to Take Over from Me — Do I Have to Wait Until This Is Resolved?

The first decision to be made is whether or not you want one or more of your children to take over. Or even whether that's an option you'd like to have in the future. If the answer is yes, then you can begin to look at alternative structures that might accomplish this.

One of the most valuable, and the most flexible, is to use a discretionary family trust as a part of the overall plan. Trusts can become complex instruments, but in essence they are quite straightforward. Historically, trusts have their origin in medieval England — it was at that time not permissible for a woman to own property in her own name, and one solution to this challenge was for a landowner/homeowner to leave the family home to a friend, who would agree to let the widow continue to live in the house for her lifetime. In this example, the homeowner would *trust* his friend to do this. It accomplished the desired end result without contravening the law at that time.

Today, a discretionary family trust is quite a popular planning tool. By way of example, suppose a business owner, John Smith, is the sole shareholder of Johnco, which has a fair market value today of $5,000,000. John and his wife, Ellen, have three children, all in their 20's, and John has no idea who might be the eventual successor. John is 50 years old and has no intention of retiring any time in the near future. One way for John to initiate the planning process without making any decisions he might regret later would be as follows:

- Set up the John Smith Family Trust, with John's mother, Jane, as the settlor (for tax reasons, it is important that John not settle the trust himself). Beneficiaries of the trust include John, Ellen, all of their children (natural or adopted) and all of their grandchildren (natural or adopted). A trust of this type is normally settled with a gold coin or some other non-income-producing asset.

- Take the common shares John now owns and exchange them for voting preferred shares in Johnco. At this point, John still owns $5,000,000 worth of Johnco shares, so, done properly, this is a non-event for tax purposes. It simply "freezes" the value of that $5,000,000 ownership interest in the company, by replacing common shares, whose value will fluctuate over time, with preferred shares, whose value is fixed at $5,000,000.

- Johnco then issues new common shares, which have only a nominal value, since the preferred shares reflect the total value of the company. The new common shares are to be owned by the John Smith Family Trust.

- Since the trust carries on no business activities and has no conventional investment assets, it receives no annual taxable income. A T3 trust income tax return has to be filed annually, but it will typically be a "nil" return.

So what does this type of structure achieve for the Smith family? The advantages are numerous and encompass most of the possible futures:

- If, 10 years from now, one of the children is running the company on a day to day basis and is the logical successor, the trust can distribute some or all of the shares to that child, ignoring the other beneficiaries. The distribution takes place on a tax-free "rollover" basis, meaning that the child takes over the shares at the same adjusted cost base as they had in the trust for tax purposes. If the value of Johnco had increased to $8,000,000 over that 10-year period, the common shares would have a value of $3,000,000, since the preferred shares are fixed at their initial $5,000,000 value.

- This effectively takes $3,000,000 of share value growth out of the capital gains tax cycle for a generation, since the entire $8,000,000 would have been taxable in John's hands if the "freeze" had not been completed, whereas it will now be taxable in the hands of the child.

- If, 10 years from now, John still has no idea who will succeed him, he can leave the shares in the trust. The time limit is a maximum of 21 years, with no minimum.

- If one of John's children becomes a "beach bum" and wants nothing to do with the world of capitalism, he or she can be excluded from any distribution.

- If a child dies, there is no disposition of shares as there would be with individual ownership — the child is a possible recipient of shares in the future, not a current shareholder.

- Similarly, if a married child goes through a divorce, there is some protection from claims of the departing spouse, since there is no current ownership.

- If a child declares bankruptcy, there is no share ownership for creditors to attach.

- In 21 years' time, it is possible that it may be appropriate to distribute shares to one or more grandchildren, even though they were mere infants at the time the trust was established. This could be done because a grandchild is a logical successor or perhaps because the children are all financially independent and the tax saving available by deferring the tax for two generations is too good to pass up.

- If, after a few years, John and Ellen decide that none of the children should be shareholders, they can then have the trust distribute the shares to them (since they are included as beneficiaries), or even to John alone, in which case the situation would look the same as it would if the "freeze" and family trust had never been completed.

- If Johnco were to be sold in the intervening years, the trust could sell its shares and would hold cash.

- Alternatively, the shares could be distributed to the three children and Ellen, since they are not already shareholders, and, assuming the shares qualify for the Small Business Gains Exemption, whereby a shareholder in a private corporation (technically a Qualifying Small Business Corporation) can, on selling or transferring shares, receive up to $500,000 in capital gains tax free.

- In this way, up to $2,500,000 of capital gains could be realized without tax ($500,000 each for John, Ellen and each of the three children). This is, of course, a very attractive tax consequence, and is facilitated by the flexibility of the trust.

All things considered, the family trust allows John and Ellen to begin to put a plan in place without sacrificing the ability to change their minds if circumstances change. Speaking of change, that's probably one of the few things we can actually count on as time passes. We know that things won't work out exactly as we would want them to, and we always need to plan in such a way that we can accommodate change as it happens. Tax rates and tax rules change, children's and parents' objectives change, business and economic climates change, technology changes, competition changes and health changes, and all of these can have an impact on any plan we put into place. Part of the advisor's job in the succession planning process is to make sure that the "what if?" questions are all asked.

I Don't Think I Want To Make My Children Wealthy. Is There an Alternative?

It is common for parents to be concerned about the impact of giving significant wealth to children. We can all think of examples where wealthy young adults have destroyed their lives via wild excesses and poor choices, and they always seem to be the ones who make front page headlines. In reality, the presence or absence of money tends not to be, in and of itself, the prime determining factor as to what kind of person someone is.

For many people, money is a magnifier — if someone is a wastrel, he/she will be a bigger wastrel with money; if someone is a good, kind person, he/she will be a better, kinder person with money. Warren Buffett, one of the world's most famous and well-respected billionaires, has said that, when it comes to children and inheritances, *you should leave them just enough so that they can do anything, but not enough so that they can do nothing.* (Indeed, in June of 2006, Buffett announced plans to donate more than $US30 billion, thus putting his philosophy into action.) This is a thought-provoking point of view, and puts things into a useful perspective. Wealth brings with it a significant responsibility, and this reinforces the need to ensure that all these issues are discussed within the family. Many children of well-to-do business owners have no idea of the extent of their parents' wealth and, while this is natural when they are very young, it can become counterproductive as they become adults. Also, the children will learn from their parents about the responsible use of wealth — to not just engage in conspicuous consumption, but also in charitable works in their community and in the country as a whole, not solely for recognition, but sometimes anonymously so that the act itself is its own reward.

Sometimes, however, no matter how much we rationalize the situation, it just doesn't seem right to leave everything to the children. So what then?

When that happens, we need to broaden the horizon a bit. Or perhaps a lot. Scott Fithian, a Boston-based financial planner and author of the superb book *Values-Based Estate Planning*,[4] spells out the process in a very effective way. When it comes to financial matters, there is a definite hierarchy, and by thinking about this hierarchy we can in essence simplify the process if it is consistent with the way we think. Fithian says that we look at financial planning issues along the following lines:

1. We strive first for financial independence.

2. Once that is achieved, then we work on providing a family legacy.

3. Only when those two are in place do we move along to providing a "Social Capital" legacy.

By "financial independence," he means the identification of a sum of money that is enough for us to live on for the rest of our lives. If, for example, someone were to determine that the amount required for financial independence is $3,000,000, then every dollar we accumulate beyond that point is surplus to actual requirements. Financial independence will include all assets, as long as they are protected in some way — for example, a 50% interest in a company worth $5,000,000 can be counted as $2,500,000 only if there is a reliably funded shareholder agreement in place, or if there is a definite plan in place that will see that interest converted to cash in the future.

Likewise, it will also include consideration of life insurance, disability insurance, critical illness insurance and long-term care insurance, since the events that would trigger the payment of any of those amounts will have an impact on the requirements of the individual and his or her immediate family.

The term "family legacy" implies, but is not restricted to, financial matters — it will also include values and priorities, personal accountability, community participation, charitable activity and spiritual beliefs.

"Social Capital" is really a measurement of the extent to which an individual's wealth exceeds the amount necessary to maintain his or her lifestyle for life and to ensure the financial well-being of the family for their lifetime. It says that once an individual has enough wealth to look after his or her own wants and needs and to look after the future wants and needs of family members, then any wealth that remains provides an opportunity for that individual to have an impact, sometimes a significant impact, on society, either by the payment of taxes (involuntary social capital) or by donations to philanthropic and charitable organizations (voluntary social capital).

---

[4] Scott Fithian, *Values-Based Estate Planning* (New York: Wiley, 2000), 20-22.

This approach results in a new way of looking at the planning process, and the questions become:

1. Do I have enough money to meet my own needs for my lifetime?

2. How much wealth should I provide for my family?

3. What do I really want to do with whatever is left over?

This directly addresses the issue of not wanting to make one's children wealthy, or at least not too wealthy, since it is not predicated on them simply inheriting whatever is left over, but rather involves a pro-active decision as to what is appropriate. It is not necessarily an easy decision to make, and usually involves many different and sometimes conflicting factors, but it generally results in a plan with which everyone can feel comfortable.

I Can See the Value of Planning for Future Ownership, but I'm Not Ready To Retire, and May Never Be Ready. How Do I Handle This?

One thing to consider is that the "old style" definition of retirement has changed fundamentally. Not so long ago, the generally accepted approach was that people would reach a certain age, typically 60 or 65, then walk away from working for a living and do nothing of substance for the rest of their lives. Today, nothing could be further from the truth, especially for business owners. Standard practice today is for business owners to start working fewer hours, perhaps fewer days per week, perhaps play more golf or spend more time fishing, or to simply take more frequent and longer vacations. As long as there is a management team in place to keep things running, this works well.

From a succession planning perspective, this raises some interesting issues:

1. It is possible that the ability to retire is a learned skill rather than a natural one. It certainly takes some effort. If a business owner typically forsakes annual vacations with his or her spouse and family, in favour of looking after the business, then leaving the business behind at some future date becomes more and more traumatic. We can all think of instances where a friend or colleague has retired and then died shortly afterwards, and this always makes us think that we should approach retirement differently if we are to succeed at succession. We need to "practice" vacationing, to take frequent vacations, even if they are short breaks rather than major trips.

2. In addition, most business owners need to retire to something rather than just retire from something. The need to work has to be replaced by something other than the option of sleeping late. In today's environment, the old standbys of golf, gardening and reading don't seem to cut it, and many "retired" business owners are busier than they ever used to be, with charitable work, mentoring, travelling, consulting and business development activities. For people who hate their jobs, retirement may still be a desirable vision of freedom, but that is by far the exception rather than the rule.

3. The financial aspect of planning for retirement is also impacted by this change in philosophy. We still tend to plan, whether with pensions or with RRSP's, that there will come a day when all other income will stop, but the succession planning process is an integral part of financial planning for retirement. Ongoing employment income is far more common than it used to be.

4. When a business owner avoids vacations and seems to be prepared to continue working forever, he or she also sends a message to senior employees, whether they are family members or not. The implied message is that they do not have the ability to run the company in his or her absence. Even worse, they are often not given the opportunity to make independent decisions or to learn from mistakes.

5. Some business owners take annual vacations grudgingly, and make a point of telephoning the office once or twice a day, just to see how things are going. Again, this implies that employees are incapable of managing without him or her. Even worse, the employees know they never really have to make a decision, since, if they wait a couple of hours, the boss is going to phone anyway, so they can wait and ask then. The final insult occurs when the boss returns from vacation and immediately wants to review everything that happened in his or her absence. This makes the succession planning process very difficult.

6. Whatever the business owner's view of retirement, the planning has to take place well in advance; otherwise, when the time comes, no one will be prepared. If he or she thinks that ongoing consulting is the preferred route, then that can be built into the plan, as we will see later. If he or she wants to remain fully involved and in control indefinitely, then that could be part of the plan, and succession would become a contingency plan (what happens in the event of a

disability or a critical illness, for example?) rather than a specific target.

If the business is to continue to survive, or even thrive, plans have to be in place to provide for what happens when the owner or founder is no longer involved, whether part-time or full-time. Simply postponing the planning aggravates the problems created, and offers no solution at all. Agreements can be designed to provide flexibility and choice, since we know that things rarely turn out exactly the way we imagine anyway. Getting the process started is always the key.

Do We Really Need the Expense of Putting Legal Agreements in Place? After All, We Are Family, We Trust Each Other.

In a close family environment, whether a natural family or a business family, it is tempting to avoid the expense of legal agreements. Generally speaking, this would be false economy. When we consider the high-profile family fights we see in the press and the lower-profile fights we get to hear about in our own communities, it is evident that family fights are often worse than fights among strangers. Legal agreements become the minimum standard of performance and in that sense offer a form of "safety net" for the plans put in place. As an example, suppose that Joe signs an agreement with Joeco that provides for an amount of $150,000 to be paid on Joe's retirement at age 65. When Joe reaches 65, it becomes evident that Joeco has fared much better than anticipated over the years, and the company offers to increase the payment to $200,000. Not surprisingly, Joe agrees, and the increased payment is made. In essence, Joe and Joeco agree to modify the agreement. Similarly, in the event that Joeco does not perform so well, they could agree to reduce the payment to $100,000, or could instead agree to spread the payment over a period of time — if Joe is the founder of the company, it is unlikely he would want to create financial hardship for the company. In the absence of a written agreement, it might be possible for a new owner to decide to spend the available cash on new machinery or to increase his or her own salary instead.

If, at the time the amount is payable, the parties to the agreement are in serious disagreement over this or other issues, or indeed if as a result they are no longer speaking to each other, then the amount in the written agreement will prevail. It acts as a form of insurance, guaranteeing the originally desired end result.

In addition, a written agreement can serve as a roadmap for a future management team. As an example, the death or permanent disability of a shareholder can result in various alternative forms of buyout, some current and some deferred. A written agreement indicates preferences and procedures, as long as it is kept up to date. As is so often the case, it is inadvisable to sign an agreement and then never consider revising it as time passes and circumstances change. When it comes time to arrange for the transfer or sale of shares, the first place a legal advisor will look for guidance will be any written agreement (as long as it is signed, which is not always the case).

My Children Don't Have the Necessary Skills To Run the Business. Do I Have To Look Outside the Family for a Successor?

There are at least two major approaches to this issue. First of all, are the skills you are looking for learnable, as opposed to innate? Can your children learn the necessary skills at a university, college or trade school? Can they learn the skills by working elsewhere? For example, a company significantly larger than yours might prove to be a good training ground and might have better training facilities. Some business owners will not allow any child to enter the family business until he or she has already worked successfully at some other business.

This is an important consideration, and can affect how other employees perceive the owner's son or daughter suddenly appearing on the scene and assuming a senior position. Having a son or daughter of the owner graduate with a bachelor's degree and then be made Vice-President, Marketing is sure to create friction among the employees, but if that son or daughter has already worked his or her way up to that position at another company, the impression conveyed is entirely different and their entry into the company much smoother.

Secondly, is it essential for your children to be able to run the business the way you do right away? Is it possible to separate ownership and management, even temporarily? For example, if a business owner's sudden death or permanent disability results in his or her inexperienced children assuming ownership of the family business, is it possible for key employees to take over management responsibilities, whether on a permanent or interim basis? If, for example, the senior engineer has worked at the company for fifteen years and knows everything about how it works, he/she knows all the contacts and all the tricks of the trade, so to speak, can he be relied on to keep the company moving forward?

Eventually, the children will gain experience and will be able to become more and more active in managing the business; initially, though, they might be owners but not managers. When there is just not enough time to get all the plans in place before the owner vanishes from the scene, this can be a useful compromise. It does, of course, require the enthusiastic cooperation of the employee or employees in question.

Another point to be made here is that you should try to take advantage of all major resources available. For example, the Canadian Association of Family Enterprise (CAFE) has excellent programs and discussion groups to facilitate exactly this kind of problem solving. Check out their website at www.cafenational.org to get in touch with a local chapter. Membership provides many benefits, and their advisory groups and "Roadmap" course can be an invaluable source of practical information in the succession process as well as in all aspects of managing a family-owned business.

Sometimes, it pays to think small. If you are not sure of the ability of a son or daughter to run the company, a helpful test can be to hand him or her a specific business project. Provide an objective, a budget, the necessary human and/or technological resources and an agreed upon method of measuring success, then step back. Don't interfere unless total disaster looms on the horizon — people need to be able to make a few mistakes, as long as they are not of the catastrophic variety. Over a period of time, the projects can become more complex, more open-ended and more central to the success or failure of the business itself. In this way, successor ownership and successor management can be grown internally on a rational, organized basis. A starting project could be a specific sales campaign, a customer appreciation event, a research project to determine new product initiatives or the launch of a new product. This exercise can be both fun and informative.

What Can I Do To Encourage Senior Employees To Stay Around When I Retire and New Ownership Takes Over?

In a great many small businesses, there are one or two key people who have been there since day one. They know all the customers, all the suppliers, all the bankers and all the other advisors. Everything. It would be difficult for any new owner of the business not to have access to their knowledge. It would be devastating if the new owners were the founder's children, who had no real business experience.

Generally speaking, loyal, long-serving employees do not work just for the money. Money is important, of course, but not all-important. One of the keys is recognition, which is not entirely monetary in nature. Sometimes, a special title, a private office, extra vacation time and similar "perks" can make all the difference.

At other times, we have to be more creative. These key employees are not owners, and would not necessarily want the responsibilities and risks that accompany ownership, but the benefits of capitalism do tend to have a strong appeal. Minority share ownership in a private company can be an inconvenience to everyone, so actual share ownership is often problematic.

There is, however, the possibility of a Share Appreciation Rights Plan, more commonly referred to as a Phantom Stock Plan. Suppose Jim, at age 50, has been with Opco for 20 years. He is well paid, but is constantly being "headhunted" for other positions. He lives a relatively modest lifestyle, and has little need for lots of extra income today, but is keen to retire at 60 rather than 65, as long as he can afford it. The business owner approaches Jim with a suggested "deal" if he agrees to stay with Opco until his retirement, regardless of changes in ownership. The deal is along the following lines:

- Present company value is around $4,000,000, based on a multiple of 6 times earnings before taxes.

- Jim will receive today a notional 5% share in the future growth in value of Opco.

- The 5% has no interim value, but will be paid in cash to Jim if he stays with Opco until a scheduled retirement date, set for when Jim reaches age 60.

- If the value of Opco has increased to $6,000,000 (based on the same multiple of earnings) by Jim's retirement date, then he is entitled to receive 5% of that $2,000,000 growth, or $100,000.

- In the event of Jim's death prior to age 60, while still in Opco's employment, his estate or named beneficiary will receive the $100,000 payment.

- In the event of Jim's total disability while employed by Opco, he will receive an income of $2,000 per month for 30 months.

- If Jim leaves Opco prior to reaching age 60, he will forfeit any entitlement to the above payments.

Obviously, this approach will not be appropriate in all cases, but it is often a useful strategy, and can go a long way toward making sure that a key employee stays and is available during a key transition period. A further advantage of the Phantom Stock Plan is that it does not require any official registration and can be applied selectively to specific key employees rather than to classes of employees, as would be the case with most pension arrangements.

Now That We're Talking About Money, How Am I Going To Get Paid for My Ownership Interest? None of the Potential Buyers Has Any Money.

When it comes to the sale of an interest in a privately held business, the general rule seems to be that you will usually get bought out with your own money. This sounds shocking, but it happens more often than not. Rarely, very rarely, a qualified, capable buyer shows up with cash, but this is certainly not something you can typically rely on. The sale of a business interest is often a series of compromises — price, terms of payment, contingency items, transition period and so on. So when you talk to a potential buyer, you should be prepared for any of the following discussions:

- Cash — A cash buyer typically wants to negotiate a lower price to reflect the convenience and desirability of a cash purchase.

- Borrowing Costs — Of course, a cash buyer may be borrowing the cash from a bank or other lender, so there is always another layer of cost to consider from the buyer's perspective. The advantage here is that the risk rests squarely on the shoulders of the buyer.

- Payment over time — Instead of a single payment of, say, $2,000,000, the buyer might offer $400,000 a year for 5 years, $500,000 a year for 4 years, or even $200,000 a year for 10 years. Usually, the longer the term is stretched out, the less desirable the offer becomes, because the risk on the part of the seller increases — what happens if the new owner runs the company into the ground after 5 years and still has 5 more payments to make? (Guarantees can be of limited value when there is absolutely no money to back them up, and the seller's only recourse might be to take back the shares in a now worthless company.)

- Staying on — The buyer might offer full asking price, but only if you agree to stay on for anywhere from one to five years. This may be acceptable, as it allows you to keep an eye on what's happening with the business and gives you the opportunity to fix problems before they become catastrophic. Of course, your salary would be payable in addition to the share purchase price. On the other hand, this type of arrangement may be unacceptable if your motivation for selling is simply to get away from the pressure of the business, to travel the world and play golf. Unless, of course, the buyer were prepared to increase the purchase price. As mentioned, a completed sale will often result from a series of compromises.

If I Plan To Sell to My Children, Do I Still Have the Same Options, or Is there More Flexibility?

Sale to a family member can be for cash or for payment over time, but there are usually other options. The ideal starting point is to look at the seller's capital and income need, then design an arrangement that addresses the best interests of both buyer and seller.

Suppose the seller of the business has no need for significant amounts of capital, but would like a secure income for life. He/she could agree to leave the business to the children by will, and simply receive dividends during his/her lifetime. To "freeze" the eventual tax liability at today's level, the owner exchanges common shares for fixed-value preferred shares, as outlined earlier in this section, then has the company issue new common shares (with a nominal value) to the children. He/she may receive dividends on the preferred shares for life. Eventually, the shares pass to the children by will, and tax will be payable on the capital gain on the share at that time. This avoids the children having to come up with large amounts of cash.

Of course, the drawback to this approach is twofold — the children have no real risk in the transaction, and the seller's position is not really protected. The seller's preferred shares have voting control, but there is little satisfaction in this if he/she has to keep an eye on things every day to make sure all is going according to plan. It boils down to how comfortable the parent/seller feels having the security of his/her life's work in the hands of one or more of the children. It sounds intimidating when expressed in those terms, but that is the issue a great many business owners face. The same issue may exist even when children are not involved, such as when there is a sale to employees, since an employee rarely has cash or even access to cash to make a purchase.

Again, a compromise may be appropriate — the children can borrow, say, $1,000,000 to provide a cash purchase price for some of the shares, and then have the same dividend structure as above. By judicious and careful share reorganization, it may be possible to provide Mom and Dad with a special block of shares worth $500,000, to allow for a purchase to take advantage of the Small Business Gains Exemption of $500,000, giving Mom and Dad a tax-free $1,000,000 start on their retirement. The $1,000,000 bank loan gives the children a stake in the process, as the loan does have to be repaid to the bank, and the bank would probably not be as benevolent and understanding as the parents in the event that payments are late or missed.

The degree to which this kind of structure makes sense is dependent on the particular circumstances. If the parents have some degree of financial flexibility, this may be appropriate, but if the slightest deviation from the plan would send them into desperation, then a different structure would be called for. As a general rule, though, there is little to be gained from having children make the full purchase price, on which the parents would pay some tax, so that the parents can eventually leave the proceeds of the purchase to the children by will, perhaps triggering another layer of tax. Income tax liability should never be the driving force behind a plan, but it does need to be included as one of the factors for consideration.

Is an Outright Sale for Cash Always the Best Thing?

There are rarely right or wrong answers to this type of question, and, as usual, everything depends on the specific situation. One way of looking at this is to ask: "If there were an outright cash sale, what would the outcome look like?" As an example, suppose Bob owns a construction business with a fair market value of $2,000,000. Bob has worked hard over the last 30 years — building the business, developing a loyal core group of reliable employees and establishing a good reputation in the community. At the age of 60, Bob needs to slow down a lot — his wife, Trish, is insisting that he take some serious time away from work, preferably sell out and walk away altogether, before his health suffers and it's too late.

Bob really wants to sell to his employees. They, of course, have no money, but they do have an entrepreneurial spirit of sorts, and they are prepared to borrow some money to make it happen. At the same time, an outside buyer is prepared to offer $1,800,000 in cash, right now, with no strings attached.

Trish's desire for a complete break form the business prompts Bob to look closely at the cash offer. As the sole shareholder, he will receive $1,800,000 in cash. Since he started the business from scratch, his original cost for his shares is $0 (it would usually be some nominal amount, but this makes the numbers easier) and the capital gain realized when he sells his shares is $1,800,000. Of this, 50% is taxable, so $900,000 taxed at 40% is $360,000. After paying the $360,000 of tax, Bob is left with $1,440,000.

For the first time in his life, Bob has cash. What should he do with it? If he invests it conservatively (definitely Trish's preference) he might earn 4%, maybe even 5%. Let's be optimistic and say he earns 5%. That would provide Bob and Trish with a pre-tax income of $72,000. But Bob has never earned less than $150,000 since as far back as he can remember. The end result is that negotiating the successful sale of his business would result in a 50% drop in his pre-tax income. If he retires today, he and Trish will have the opportunity to take all the vacation trips they never had time for, but at this rate they won't have the income to be able to afford them.

Bob has a friend who says he should be able to earn a conservative 15% on his money. This would make the pre-tax income $216,000, which is much better, more along the lines of what Bob and Trish were hoping for, but of course this introduces significant risk into the formula — how realistic is a 15% rate of return on a regular, sustainable basis?

The key here is that Bob ceases to be an entrepreneur and, at age 60, becomes an investor for the first time in his life. It is crucial that Bob should receive some solid investment advice from someone he trusts. It is possible that he might also have to face the fact that the typical sale is not likely to provide him with what he wants. So what about the employees?

Suppose a group of employees get together and agree to come up with $500,000 as a down payment. Assuming the shares qualify for the capital gains exemption and that the corporate structure is conducive to this, the $500,000 could all be tax free, and Bob could invest it however he and Trish agree to. The remaining $1,500,000 of the purchase price could be deferred, perhaps indefinitely, in exchange for interest payments. Perhaps dividends could be paid. Perhaps consulting fees could be added to the mix. Perhaps insurance on Bob's life could guarantee purchase of the shares on his death so that Trish would no longer be dependent on the ongoing viability of the business.

Would this produce a better end result? Might it provide more income? It becomes a simple matter of analysis, but we cannot ignore the increased risk. Whereas the original 15% investment plan had significant investment risk, this revised approach might have significant business risk. From an income point of view, there is no such thing as being risk-free. A 4% investment return might be guaranteed, but there is a risk that it is simply not enough for Bob and Trish to live on comfortably. As we said earlier, it is always a matter of compromise, and we have to recognize that the perfect solution might not exist.

Creativity is the order of the day.

As We Go Through the Planning Process, What Are Some of the Pitfalls We Have To Watch Out for?

- In Canada, we do not have succession duty, estate tax or gift tax, as these were all abolished when the taxation of capital gains began in 1972. This is not true in the United States, however, and care should be taken to ensure that you do not unwittingly have an unanticipated tax liability in the U.S. All citizens of the United States have a liability for estate tax on their worldwide assets, regardless of their country of residence or the location of the assets, even if they are also citizens of another country, such as Canada. (The U.S. authorities do not officially recognize the dual citizenship issue — the only question is whether an individual is or is not a U.S. citizen.) This may be an issue if you have U.S. citizenship, if your children are U.S. citizens or live in the U.S., or if you retire to the U.S. (yes, including Hawaii) — do you want your children to be shareholders in your family business if it is going to create future tax problems?

- In addition, Canadian citizens or Canadian residents who are citizens of other countries may have U.S. estate tax liability on U.S. assets, which would include, for example, shares in Microsoft or IBM, along with any real estate located in the U.S. That condo in Maui might have a significant tax liability attached to it.

- There has been a move for the U.S. to abandon the estate tax altogether — indeed, legislation has been passed calling for its end in 2010 — but the general feeling among U.S. tax practitioners is that the legislation will be amended and the tax will survive in some form.

- One of the common obstacles to tax-efficient planning is a failure to have an appropriate corporate structure to take advantage of the capital gains exemption, or, even better, to multiply the exemption in the hands of other family members.

- Paradoxically, another obstacle is to try too hard to set up for maximum capital gains exemptions, so that the end result, as well as being expensive, is completely unintelligible to the people for whose benefit it was intended.

- At times, going too far down the planning road before getting input from other stakeholders creates problems. It is advisable to get other people involved as soon as you can.

The biggest problem in succession planning comes from leaving it until too late. Having a clear direction and objective in mind, even if it's many years away, can help determine corporate structure, share ownership, management remuneration, family communication and all aspects of financial and retirement planning. It is not difficult to find a great deal of help, but it becomes an uphill battle if you start too late, no matter how successful the business may be.

It is possible to have two virtually identical businesses, in the same geographic location, in the same type of business, with the same annual earnings, the same type of workforce and the same level of customer goodwill, yet for one business to have a significantly better chance of long-term survival with the next generation of owners and beyond, simply because of the way it has organized itself, conducted its business and handled its relationship with its customers. Ultimately, that business will command a better price, will provide better service to its customers and will offer a more secure retirement for its founding shareholders. It all comes down to advance preparation.

A Business Succession Planning Checklist

Potential Successors

- ❏ Partner/shareholder
- ❏ Family member
- ❏ Employee
- ❏ Competitor
- ❏ Outsider

Family Priorities

- ❏ Harmony
- ❏ Equality
- ❏ Fairness
- ❏ Create family legacy

Personal Priorities

- ❏ Comfortable retirement income
- ❏ Minimize taxes
- ❏ Maximize philanthropy
- ❏ Preserve wealth for children/grandchildren
- ❏ Spend everything
- ❏ Ensure business survival
- ❏ Never retire
- ❏ Always to be needed
- ❏ Standing in the community

Business Topics

- ❏ CCPC?
- ❏ QSBC?
- ❏ SBGE used? Available?
- ❏ SBGE multiplication a possibility?
- ❏ Holding company appropriate?

❏ Debt insured?

❏ Shareholder agreement in force? Current? Funded?

❏ Personal guarantees outstanding

❏ Retention of key employees

❏ Employee incentive plans

❏ Voting control

   (i) Who?

   (ii) When to change?

Retirement

❏ When?

❏ Full or partial retirement?

❏ Who takes over?

❏ Need capital or income?

❏ Safe to leave capital in business?

❏ Insurance funding?

❏ Individual Pension Plan?

❏ Retirement Compensation Arrangement?

Death or Disability

❏ Who takes over? When?

❏ For how much?

❏ Tax liability

❏ Insurance funding

❏ Spouse free from dependence on business?

Shareholder Agreement

❏ Signed?

❏ Valuation procedure

❏ Triggering events defined?

❏ Grandfathered for stop-loss rules?

❏ Permit share transfer to holding company?

❏ Cross-purchase or corporate share repurchase?

❏ Hybrid

❏ Use of Capital Dividend Account

❏ Life insurance funding

   (i) Regular review?

   (ii) Amount and type

   (iii) Handling of shortfall

❏ Provision for disability?

❏ Exposure to creditors

❏ Maintaining insurance after retirement

❏ Revise to reflect estate freeze?

   (i) Make sure correct parties included

   (ii) Include all classes of shares

Tax Issues

❏ U.S. citizenship?

   (i) Income tax

   (ii) Estate tax

   (iii) Gift tax

❏ Canadian citizens

   (i) U.S. Estate tax on U.S. property

   (ii) Beware "dual" citizenship problems

Stakeholders to Consult

❏ Employees

❏ Family members

❏ Suppliers

- ❏ Customers
- ❏ Lenders
- ❏ Advisors
- ❏ Shareholders

TOPICAL INDEX